Charles Stewart

Gaelic Kingdom in Scotland, its Origin and Church

With Sketches of Notable Breadalbane and Glenlyon Saints

Charles Stewart

Gaelic Kingdom in Scotland, its Origin and Church
With Sketches of Notable Breadalbane and Glenlyon Saints

ISBN/EAN: 9783743419070

Manufactured in Europe, USA, Canada, Australia, Japa

Cover: Foto ©Lupo / pixelio.de

Manufactured and distributed by brebook publishing software (www.brebook.com)

Charles Stewart

Gaelic Kingdom in Scotland, its Origin and Church

THE

GAELIC KINGDOM IN SCOTLAND

Its Origin and Church

WITH SKETCHES OF NOTABLE BREADALBANE
AND GLENLYON SAINTS

By CHARLES STEWART

EDINBURGH: MACLACHLAN & STEWART
LONDON: SIMPKIN, MARSHALL, & CO.

MDCCCLXXX

PREFACE.

OUR early history has usually been written from the statements of the old chroniclers, compared with the scanty notices to be found in the Latin authors. As so written, it is more the conclusions of the historian's own subjectivity, exercised on these ancient documents, than results drawn from undoubted facts. The chroniclers wrote centuries after the circumstances recorded took place, so that really the foundation of the records was unwritten tradition, and therefore to a considerable extent apocryphal. The Romans, again, in writing of the Gaelic kingdom, were dealing with a people amongst whom they never got a footing, and of whom they could only have a very imperfect knowledge. We have, however, a source of information in floating tradition, which our historians have looked upon with great contempt, but which, notwithstanding, has usually a real element of truth in it. Also we have monuments, usages, customs, and names, all of which, when carefully and cautiously questioned, throw a flood of light on the other evidences. These have been very much neglected.

In reference to the old Gaelic names, it is necessary to object in the strongest manner to the interpretation of these, from the mere sound or seeming suitableness of the words, by those who know nothing of the history of the monuments or places, which they so presumptuously undertake to elucidate. Such amateur displays of paraded ignorance have done painful injury to Celtic inquiries.

In the following pages I have endeavoured to combine these sources of evidence, and to make the one throw light on the other. With what success my readers must judge. I can at least plead an intimate knowledge of the customs, language, lore, and monuments of my native district.

TIGHNDUIN, BY KILLIN, 1880.

TABLE OF CONTENTS.

CHAPTER I.

ORIGIN OF THE GAELIC KINGDOM.

	PAGE
Albin; Scotia, Scots, and Scotland; early races,	1
Gothic races, their route from Asia,	2
Brettonich or Britons; Albanich,	3
Gaidhill or Gaels,	4
Gaidhill-dhonn or Caledonians; Feinne or Fenians,	6
Fingal; Dhubh-gall; Fion-gall,	7
Gall-n-Gaoidheal; Scuittich or Scots; Mic-Milidh or Milesians; founding of Gaelic kingdom at an early date,	8
Theodosius; Claudian,	9
Gaelic kingdom prior to Romans,	11
Gaelic kingdom coeval with Romans,	12
Scots and Picts separate kingdoms,	13
Scots and Picts united under Kenneth M'Alpin; Cruithnich or Picts,	15
Sluagh Fea,	16

CHAPTER II.

THE CELTIC CHURCH IN THE GAELIC KINGDOM.

Prelacy and Episcopacy distinguished,	19
Celtic Church non-prelatic,	20
Value of Bede, Cummian, and Adamnan as chroniclers,	21
Difference in beliefs and usages of Celtic and Roman Churches; Celtic monasteries presided over by Presbyter Abbats,	24

vi *Table of Contents.*

	PAGE
Episcopal "function" untenable,	27
Irish-Roman monasteries presided over by bishops,	28
Founding of Roman Church in Scotland,	29
Origin of Celtic Church in Britain and Scotland,	30
Revival of religion in sixth century,	32
Irish monasteries; Celtic and Roman different,	33
Columba's coming to Ii; Celtic bishop ordained by elders for Northumbria,	34
Reverse to Celtic Church, eighth century,	36
Persecution by Malcolm, Margaret, and David,	37
Revival of Celticism at Reformation; survival of Druidic beliefs,	39

CHAPTER III.

MONASTERY OF II AND ST COLUMBA.

Different work assigned to monks,	40
Bishops; scribe; ferleighinn; two orders anchorites,	41
Deorich or Dewars,	42
Cuildich or Culdees; cuile, different significations,	43
Calledei; Gille-Dhe; Gille-Christ,	47
Gille-Faolan; Deicolæ; Christicolæ; Celechrist; Columba,	48
John Knox,	48 and 52

CHAPTER IV.

EASTERN BREADALBANE AND AIDIN

Innis-Aidin; Kenmore; Aidin's friendship with Donald Breac,	53
Mission to Northumbria; King Oswald interpreting; character depicted,	54
Part of remains deposited at Innis-Aidin,	56

CHAPTER V.

FORTINGALL AND ST CEODE.

Topography,	57
Roman defeat; St Fiachre,	58
St Ciaran,	59
St Ceode, patron saint of Fortingall,	60

Table of Contents. vii

	PAGE
St Chad, patron saint of Logierait,	61
Removal to Northumbria; Ceode, bishop of East Saxons; Chad, bishop of York and Lichfield,	62
Ceode founds monastery of Lestingau,	65

CHAPTER VI.

GLENLYON AND EONAN.

Topography,	69
Central seat of Feinne; remains of castles, &c.,	70
Balnahannait; worship of Annait in Asia and Egypt,	72
Monuments, worship, and rites in Gaelic kingdom,	73
Proof Central Asia cradle of Feinne; Annaits places of Celtic worship,	74
Celtic Church bell found at Balnahannait; Eonan, patron saint of Glenlyon; his prayers and funeral,	75
Cladh Bhrainnu; Cladh-Ghunnaidh,	76

CHAPTER VII.

FAOLAN OF WESTERN BREADALBANE.

Kentigerna, Congan, and Faolan landing at Lochalsh; coming to Strathfillan,	78
Faolan under vows as a Deoraich; reputed miracles,	79
Preaching places; meal mill; fair,	80
Death; funeral,	81
Holy pool; relic at Bannockburn,	82
Faolan of Strathearn different person,	83

CHAPTER VIII.

FAOLAN'S RELICS.

Crozier,	85
Coigreach; Coighmheurach; Faraichd,	86
Deoraich originally a family name,	87
Faolan their probable ancestor; Euich; Bell,	88
Healing stones,	89

CHAPTER XI.

FEINNE OR GAIDHILL.

	PAGE
Gall misinterpreting *Gaidhill*,	90
Three kinds bardic remains,	91
Sgeulachds ethical ; Gaidhill emotional ; intellectually thorough,	92
Paulinism or predestination, how believed in,	93
Belief in oneness of present and future life,	94
Conception of music ; mission of bards,	95
Pipe music, whence its power,	96
Demeanour of Gaidhill in battle,	97
Crith-gaisge ; mir-cath,	98

APPENDIX.

Feinne not a militia but a people,	99
Tests as to personal residence of saints,	100
Ecclesiastical terms not necessarily from Latin,	101

ERRATUM.

Page 25, line 16 from top, *for* "Strathfillan" *read* "Glendochart."

The Gaelic Kingdom of Scotland.

CHAPTER I.

ORIGIN OF THE GAELIC KINGDOM IN PERTHSHIRE, ARGYLESHIRE, AND INVERNESS-SHIRE.

THE first name of Scotland was Albin. The names Scotia and Scots for the first ten centuries were most frequently applied to Ireland and the Irish. It was only after Malcolm Ceanmore came to the throne in the eleventh century that Albin came to be usually known as Scotland. Long before that, however, part of its inhabitants, as we shall afterwards see, were known as Scots. We find that Great Britain was originally peopled by three principal races, viz.,—(1) Brettonich, or Britons; (2) Gaidhill, known also as Feinne, Scuittich, and Mic-Milidh; and (3) Cruithnich, or Picts. These races were all of Celtic origin, and had their source in Asia. From thence they passed to Europe, chiefly by the Hellespont, and so onwards through Greece, Macedonia, Italy, France, and Belgium, until, having reached the sea, some of their utmost tribes took ship and crossed over to Great Britain and Ireland. Without doubt it would be the most enterprising that did this;

so that at our very beginning we sprung from those whose inherent characteristics were daring endeavour and hardy bearing. The Gothic races, who also came from Asia, took a more northerly route than the Celtic, and so passed onwards to Germany and Scandinavia. Tradition points strongly to Asiatic Scythia as the cradle of the Celtic races; and this is confirmed by the ancient language of all those countries where they had settlements, and by the names of towns, rivers, mountains, and other developed and natural features most prominent in these lands.

It is necessary to premise that, besides the generic name or names, each of these races contained within it many tribes, and that the Romans did not always comprehend their distinguishing names and characteristics. Thus, for instance, we find Ammianus making Picts both of the Vecturiones and Dicaledonii. Now, we know that, whilst the former were Picts, the latter were a Gaelic tribe. In contradistinction to Ichturiones or *Iochdarich*—that is, inhabitants of the low lands,—Vecturiones or *Uachdarich* were the inhabitants of the higher lands. Their district can still be traced under the name of *Druim-Uachdar* in the braes of Athole and Badenoch. The Dicaledonii in Gaelic are styled *Dubh-Gaidhill;* that is, Gaidhill or Gaels of purest and most unmixed descent,—the prefix *Dubh* being very commonly used in the sense of quintessence or thoroughness. Their district lay in the Highlands of Perthshire, marching with *Druim-Uachdar.*

It must also be noted that the Romans had somewhat indefinite conceptions of those parts of Albin into which they had either not penetrated at all, or penetrated only in a very sporadic fashion. We find traces of such temporary occupation at Fortingall through the Tay valley, and at Bochastle through the Teith valley; but into the great Highlands beyond, on the north and west, they never pierced at all. We must, therefore, expect to find inaccurate statements in their topography of these regions.

I will now take up the history of each of these three principal races separately, and

I. THE BRITONS.

The Britons in Gaelic are styled *Brettonich*. They seem to have been the first race that peopled Great Britain. The "Pictish Chronicle" says they came in the third age of the world. This, according to the "Historia Britonum," ascribed to Nennius, would be from the time of Abraham to David. The *Sluagh Fea*, or *Fidhbha*, who were exterminated by the Picts, are the only British tribe that we read of in Ireland. That the Britons were a Celtic race is undoubted, both from the remains of the language, and the ancient names in England and parts of Scotland. We have in the chroniclers the legend that they were a Roman colony, who, under a chief named Brutus, took possession of the country, and which he divided into three kingdoms, bestowing one upon each of his three sons. These kingdoms were Briton, now England; Cumry, now Wales; and Albin, now Scotland. This cannot be true in all its extent, as, if these were simply Romans, the language would have been Latin, and not Gaelic. It is extremely likely, however, to be true thus far, that there were three British kingdoms, as above described. The first king of the northern portion was, we are told, Albanach, or, Latinised, Albanactus, evidently from the Gaelic word *banach*, or the fair one. It is further said that the kingdom took its name of Albin from him. I think, however, that the statement in the "Pictish Chronicle," which says that the name had its origin not from the characteristics of one individual, but from those of the whole race, is much more probable. That they were a fair-haired and complexioned race is certain.

The preface *alb* may be from the old word signifying high, in which case *Albanich* means the tall fair race.

It appears further from the chroniclers that their progress from Asia was first to Italy, then to Bretagne in France, and from thence to Britain. They peopled the whole of England and Wales, and the southern, eastern, and northern parts of Scotland, then called Albin. It appears, however, that they got no footing in those parts of the Highlands which afterwards formed the Gaelic kingdom. This conclusion we arrive at from the fact that there is nowhere to be found in this latter any remains of names in the British dialect, such as are to be found in other parts of Scotland.

The inhabitants of the Scottish Lowlands are descendants of the Britons. With this British race, however, there has mingled a very large Saxon element, and in a smaller degree that of the Dane and Norman.

It may be mentioned that either Aristotle himself, who flourished in the third century B.C., or his disciple Theophrastus, who edited his works, speaks both of Albium and Brettania.

II. THE GAIDHILL.

The Gaidhill—in English, the Gaels; in Latin, Caledonii—are known to us by three other names :—The Feinne (English, Fenians); the Scuittich (English, Scots); and Mic-Milidh (English, Milesians). Thus in the Irish and Pictish additions to Nennius we find the old chronicler saying :—

"What was the land in which they lived,
Lordly men, the Fene ?
What brought them for want of land
To the setting of the sun ?

"What is the proper name for them
As a nation,
By which they were called in their own country,
Scuitt or Gaedhil.

> "Why was Fene said to be
> A name for them?
> And Gaedhil—which is the better,
> Whence was it derived?
>
> "What adventure were they upon
> In their angry course?
> Or what sons of the sons of Milidh
> Are they to be traced to?"

The part of Albin occupied by this race, and which formed the old Gaelic kingdom, consisted of Argyleshire, Lochaber, with adjoining Highlands of Inverness-shire, and the Highlands of Perthshire, including Rannoch, Glenlyon, and Breadalbane. They were undoubtedly Celts, and of cognate race to the Cruithnich or Picts. The legend as related by the chroniclers is, that Gaidhil, prince of Athens, married Scota, princess of Egypt, with whom he and his followers took ship, and reached Spain and Portugal, where he died. His sons, in obedience to his instructions, passed onwards, until they came to the eastern coast of Ireland, where they and their people settled. It also appears, as will be afterwards shown, that they made a simultaneous settlement on the west coast of Albin. On analysis what seems to be undoubted in the legend is, that this Celtic Asiatic race in their progress westwards passed through Greece, and by Spain, Portugal, and France, until they finally settled in Ireland and Albin. The name Portugal, or Port-nan-Gaidhill, is in this connection suggestive.

It will be interesting to consider separately the four different names by which this race was known, and I shall first take that of Gaidhill. This is the name by which the modern Highlander invariably designates himself. It probably comes from the word *geal*, or white, and, therefore, has the same meaning as *banach*, from which *Albanach*. Both words, *Gaidhil* and *Albanach*, denote a fair-complexioned people, and which evidently all the Celtic races were. The Latin form of the word is *Caledonii*. Many fanciful derivations of this word have been given, but it is quite unnecessary to seek so far, for, bearing in view that "G" and "C" are commutable sounds, a Highlander's pronunciation of *Gaidhil* and a Roman's of *Cale* are almost identical. To this was added the epithet *donn, i.e.,* brown. The term would then be *Gaidhill-dhonn*—or in its underived form *Geal-dhonn*—meaning a race with fair complexion and hair, verging towards brown or auburn.* The pronunciation of Caledonii, in which no doubt the Romans followed the Gaelic, shows it to be a *compounded* word, as no *uncompounded* word in that language has the accent on the last syllable. The designation of Gaidhill was originally restricted to the inhabitants of the Gaelic kingdom, but after its union with the Pictish kingdom, in the ninth century, it became the general name of the two conjoined races.

The second name by which this race was known is *Fionn*—plural *Feinne,* or, as the chronicler has it, *Fene.* The peculiarity of fairness of complexion, as already said, seems to adhere to all these Celtic races. Thus we have the Britons styled Albanach from *banach*, the Gaidhil taking his name from *geal*, and the *Fionn* from a third word used in Gaelic for white, and which has the exact same spelling as the racial term, viz., *Fionn.* Considering the remarkable similarity betwixt the religious beliefs and rites of the ancient Gaidhill and the Phœnicians, it is impossible not to have suggested to us by this racial name some connection of the two peoples. It is even probable that we owe the kilt to this relationship, as we find that "a tomb-painting of Thothmes III. represents Kefa, or Phœnicians, clad in

---

* See Alexander and Donald Stewart's "Highland Bards," p. 473-74; M'Firbis's "Genealogies," quoted in O'Curry's "Lectures," p. 223; and Tacitus's "Life of Agricola," c. xi.

richly-bordered kilts." In the Highlands of Perthshire, and the same is true of the others, whilst we invariably *now* speak of ourselves as *Gaidhill*, we as invariably speak of our ancestors as the Feinne. The lore poured into our ears since infancy has been full of them, and every spot almost on which our eye rests reminds us of them. Thus from my windows I can see *Cille'-n-fheinne* (Killin), or their burial-place; *Feinnlarig*, or their pass; and *Feinn-ghlean*, or their glen. Multiplied other instances might be given. Nothing has so darkened the real origin and history of the Feinne as the constant misuse of the word "Fingal." It has been continually used as the name of *one* individual, from whom the race were called "Fingallians," whereas it is simply descriptive, as all names then were, and signified the *Fionn-geal*, or a Fionn distinguished, even amongst a fair race, by the exceptional whiteness of his mien and complexion.* It was without doubt applied to many a Fionn besides the renowned king of Morven. As to the word Fingallian, nothing can be more absurd; it has no existence in Gaelic, and no sense in English. To us who have been all our lives, by eye and by ear, drinking in the existence and exploits of this people, it is intensely interesting to find these confirmed by the old chroniclers. This name crops up very unexpectedly amongst the bands of Northmen which, in the 9th and following centuries, infested Ireland and the western coasts of Scotland. One of these tribes was called by the Irish annalists the *Dubh-gall*, and the other the *Fion-gall*. The word *gall* means stranger; and the prefix *dubh*, as already explained, gives intensity, making *Dubh-gall* to mean utter strangers. This tribe were probably Goths. The other tribe more nearly concerns our inquiry, and means *stranger* of the *cognate* or *Fionn* race, and who doubtless

* See Gillies's "Collection," p. 41, verse 3, where he is called "Fionn-a-Chruthghil."

were Celts.* That this is the true meaning of the word is amply proved by the synonymous name, Gall-n-Gaiodheal (or, as we would spell it, *Gall-Gaidhill*), given to the same Northmen, as we find in the "Fragments of Irish Annals." This is simply using the word *Gaidhill* in connection with *Gall*, instead of its equivalent *Fionn*. And, in still further proof, the fragments go on to use the third equivalent, *Scots*. "They were Scots," they say, "and foster-children of the Northmen, and at one time used to be called Northmen." The proof is complete; these Northmen were called *Fiongall, Gall-Gaidhill*, and *Scots*,—*Fionn, Gaidhil,* and *Scot* alike signifying the same Celtic race, as this statement of the annalists, amongst others, abundantly shows, therein also confirming the statement already quoted from the additions to Nennius.

The third name by which this race was known is that of Scuittich, or Scots. It is probably the same as Scythian, and both are probably derived from *Scaoite*, or Nomads. It was used in Ireland at an early period, and, as we will see immediately, was applied to the inhabitants of the Gaelic kingdom in Albin, long before the Roman period.

The fourth name of this race was Mic-Milidh, or Milesians. It seems to have been entirely confined to the Irish Gaidhill. In the Irish and Pictish additions to Nennius, we find Herimon or Erimon, king of the Irish Gaidhill, called a *Maccaib Milidh*. We are also told that the Cruithnich, who conquered a great part of Albin, sent to Ireland for wives from the *Mic-Milidh*, and we know that it was the Gaidhill who gave them wives, leaving it in no doubt that the Gaidhill and Mic-Milidh were the same race.

There is great difference of opinion as to when the Gaelic kingdom was first established in Albin. Eminent authori-

* Probably "the Fir-bolg," who took possession "of Manand . . . Ara, and Ila and Recca," afterwards known as "Siol Cuinn," from whom the Lords of the Isles.

ties have placed it about the end of the fifth century, when Fergus Mor Mac-Erc came from Ireland and reigned over the Gaidhill of Albin in Dalriada. One very high authority (Skene) makes an exception for a short period, from A.D. 360 to 369, during which he says the Scots had a settlement in Albin, and from whence they were driven at the latter period by Theodosius. For this settlement in 360 I can find no authority. Their expulsion to Ireland in 369 he rests on the testimony of Claudian, a poet who wrote about fifty years later, who probably knew very little of the topography of Argyleshire or Ireland, and who cannot be quoted as of much authority in the matter. The Scottish Gaidhill were in the wont of sending help in time of need to their Irish kinsfolk, and the Irish in like manner to the Scots of Albin; and there may be this amount of truth in Claudian's statement, that such Irish auxiliaries returned to their own country; and who, on reporting their great losses, caused weeping and wailing in Ireland. In any case Claudian's statement cannot be twisted into asserting the expulsion of the Gaidhill from Albin to Ireland. In magnifying Theodosius he says of his victories :—

"The Orkney Isles were soaked
With Saxon blood, Thule was warmed with that of Picts,
Icy Hibernia wept the heaps of her slain Scots."

Taking this in conjunction with the title he gives Theodosius, " Conquerer of the Coasts of Britain," it can only mean that he reached Orkney and Shetland, where he made great slaughter, and either did the same in Ireland, or, as stated above, caused great havoc amongst her warriors, who fought with their brother Scots of the Gaelic kingdom of Scotland. The epithet icy, applied to Ireland, shows the ignorance of the country in which he wrote; whilst peopling Orkney and Shetland with Saxons and Picts may be mere rhetorical rodomontade.

We have ample proof that there was a Gaelic kingdom in Albin coeval with the Romans; and proof almost as certain that it was founded at that earlier period when the Gaidhill made their settlement in Ireland. In fact, the two settlements in Ireland and in Albin seem to have been made at the same time, and in Albin at least they formed the original inhabitants of the Gaelic kingdom. For this early founding of the kingdom our proof is threefold :—
(1) The unquestioned tradition of its people, that their remotest ancestors were the Feinne or Gaidhill, and who have ever since possessed it. There is not a single trace that any other historic race preceded them ; nor remains of either British or Pictish languages that I know of; (2) the perfect confirmation of this by the ancient names of places, natural objects, and monumental remains ; and (3) the statements of the chroniclers.

I will first consider the statements of the chroniclers in proof of this earlier kingdom. Bede, indeed, speaks as if the Scots came to Albin after the Picts, but in this he is contradicted by other chroniclers. The "Historia Britonum," ascribed to Nennius, says that "the Scots, 1002 years before Christ, when the Egyptians were lost in the Red Sea, passed into Ireland and the district of Dalrietta." If this latter was in Ireland, and not the Dalriada of Scotland, the sentence is meaningless, as it distinctly points to some other place not in Ireland. But Nennius leaves the matter in no doubt, for he makes the further statement that the Scots and Picts incessantly attacked the Britons a long interval before " the Romans obtained possession of the empire of the world." The "Chronicle of the Picts and Scots" is to the same effect. It says that from the massacre of the Picts in the time of Drust, " the kingdom of the Picts failed, which had lasted 1187 years, and the kingdom of the Scots recommenced, which had commenced before the Picts 443 before the Incarnation." In another place it says "the sum of the years of the reign of the Scots before the Picts was 305 years and three months."

These statements of the chroniclers are verified by the fact apparent from their early historians, that a great and powerful *Gaelic* or Caledonian kingdom existed when the Romans first reached Scotland. This implies its existence for a lengthened period previously; for it is impossible to suppose that a kingdom recently established would be strong enough, as this was, to face the Romans in an undeniably indecisive battle, and to prevent their finding any prominent footing within its borders. Agricola invaded Scotland about the year A.D. 80, and his campaigns are related to us by his nephew Tacitus, whose notices are the earliest we have by any Roman historian regarding the native population. Not having been in Britain himself, the particulars must have been supplied by his uncle. He is at sea, as all the early Roman writers were, as to the distinctive names of the tribes and sub-tribes, and classes the inhabitants under the general name of Britons. The name, however, that he gives the country is *Caledonia*, and the enemies who opposed Agricola were the men of Caledonia. Ptolemy, who wrote his geographical notices about A.D. 120, calls the race *Caledonii;* assigns to them the part of the country occupied by the Gaelic kingdom, and by the extent of territory he shows as belonging to them, manifestly considers them to be the most powerful of the native tribes. Our next authority of value is Dio Cassius, who wrote A.D. 230. In his writings we find the Caledonians to be as powerful a race as ever. He says that "when the Caledonians prepared to defend the *Meatae*, and Severus was intent on the border war, Verrius Lupus was obliged to purchase a peace from the *Meatae* at a great price." This shows what weight a threat from them carried, and also that their borders extended to the wall betwixt the Firths of Forth and Clyde. The *Meatae* are evidently the *Meadhonaiteach*, or "middle people" between the two walls; and from this extract it appears that the very preparation to help them by their northern neighbours caused the Romans to sue for peace at a great price. The statements therefore of the chroniclers and of the early Roman historians alike show that there was a Gaelic kingdom in Scotland long before the advent of the Romans. In fact, the statements of the early historians become transparent and easy of solution when we realise that the *Feinne*, *Scots*, or *Gaidhill* were one and the same people, the latter term being Latinised by the Romans into *Caledonii*.

The argument for a Gaelic or Scottish kingdom coeval with the Romans is still stronger, for, besides the proof for the earlier kingdom already adduced, we have further proof from the chroniclers, and the confirmation of the Roman historian, Ammianus. The proof for this coeval kingdom from the chroniclers is as follows :—Nennius states that the Emperor Severus ordered a wall to be "built betwixt the Britons and the Scots and the Picts," for "the Scots from the west and the Picts from the north unanimously made war against the Britons, but were at peace amongst themselves." This gives a Gaelic or Scoto kingdom in the west of Albin in the first half of the third century, and is in entire conformity with the statement of Ossian in "Comala" and "Carric-thura" that the Feinne, under their renowned leader the *Fionn-geal*, fought at the battle of Carron against the Romans under Caracalla, son of Severus. Gildas tells us that, in the time of Maximus, Britain groaned "under the cruelty of two foreign nations, the Scots from the northwest and the Picts from the north." A legion, he says, was sent from Rome, who drove these "cruel enemies beyond the borders," and gave advice to the Britons to build a wall to keep them out. The description given is accurate, leaving no doubt that the wall meant was the turf-wall between the Firths of Clyde and Forth. Bede entirely confirms this, and explains what is meant by foreign nations. He says, "from that time (about the beginning of the fourth century) the south part of Britain suffered many years under two foreign nations, the Scots from the west and the Picts from the north. We call these foreign nations, not on account of their being seated out of Britain, but because they were remote from that part of it which was possessed by the Britons; two inlets of the sea lying between them." And then he goes on to show that these were the firths of Clyde and Forth. The Picts are equally called "foreign" as the Scots; and if our historians from this term relegate the Scots to Ireland, they must also relegate the Picts. This plainly shows that Bede's explanation as to both is right. We find the same statement in Ethelwerd's "Chronicle." "Whilst," it says, "the people of Britain were living carelessly within the wall which had been built by Severus to protect them, there arose two nations—the Picts in the north and the Scots in the west— and leading an army against them, devastated their country."

Let us now see how thoroughly Ammianus, the Roman historian, confirms these statements of our old chroniclers. He says—"But the next year (A.D. 360), that of Constantine's tenth and Julian's third consulship, the affairs of Britain became troubled, in consequence of the incursions of the savage nations of Picts and Scots, who, breaking the peace to which they had agreed, were plundering the districts on their borders, and keeping in constant alarm the provinces exhausted by former disasters." It will be noticed that he distinctly says that the borders of the Scots as well as of the Picts were adjoining to the Roman provinces. He never would have so spoken if their borders were on the other side of the Irish Channel; nor yet does he say that these borders were recently acquired, but, on the contrary, speaks exactly in the same way as he does of those of the Picts. Again, he tells us that, in 369, Theodosius routed and vanquished the various tribes, and "entirely restored the cities and fortresses which, through the manifold disasters of the time, had been injured and destroyed, though they had been originally provided to secure the tranquillity of the country." "So," he goes on to say, "he restored cities and fortresses as we have already mentioned, and established stations and out-posts on our frontiers; and he so completely recovered the province which had yielded subjection to the enemy, that, through his agency, it was brought under the authority of its legitimate ruler, and from that time forth was called Valentia." Valentia was the province between the two walls; and what is evidently meant is, that Theodosius drove the Picts and Scots beyond the Forth and Clyde wall, the fortresses of which, with the cities to the south of it, he restored. There is not the slightest hint that he drove the Scots to Ireland, but perfectly the reverse. In fact, his statements are quite plain to the effect that the Scots on the west, and the Picts on the north, bordered with the Romans at the Forth and Clyde and the wall between them, and that they were driven by Theodosius beyond these, and the wall with its fortresses repaired.

When to this unanimous witness of the old chroniclers, confirmed by the Roman historian, is added the unquestioned and universal tradition of the kingdom, that the *Feinne* are our only remote ancestors; the topographical proof from the ancient names; the monumental, such as castles, watchtowers, &c.; and the fact that there are remains of no other Celtic language or dialect of language, we have, I think, proof which is complete and thorough that there existed a Gaelic or Scotic kingdom coeval with the Romans.

The proof for the earlier and original kingdom is not so full, as it wants the confirmation of Bede; but still, resting as it does on the witness of other chroniclers, the earliest Roman historians, and on that of tradition, names, monuments, and language, I think it is perfectly ample and sufficient to warrant an undoubted belief in its existence. The different kinds of proof, it will be noticed, are quite independent; and whilst one of them standing by itself might leave a doubt, the whole put together, and arriving at the same result, seems to be irrefragable.

Even in the case of Fergus Mor Mac-Erc, when we consider the close connection and constant inter-marriages betwixt the *Gaidhill-Erinnach* and the *Gaidhill-Albanach*, it is far more natural to suppose that he succeeded to the Dalriad kingdom by right of descent, and not by conquest. For in the latter case it is not the least likely that he could so shortly after his accession, as we know he did, have consolidated so large and powerful a kingdom.

The history of the Gaelic kingdom after Fergus's accession about the year 498 may be shortly stated. For more than three hundred years they lived in a state of rivalry to the Picts, until at length, in the ninth century, the two kingdoms were united into one under Kenneth M'Alpin. And from which time the united peoples came to be known as *Gaidhill*.

III. CRUITHNICH OR PICTS.

The third great race of Celts were the Cruithnich, called Picts by the Romans, from their custom of tatooing and staining their bodies. This Latin word was used first by Eumenius the Rhetorician, in an oration in praise of Constantius Chlorus, A.D. 296. We find from a subsequent oration, A.D. 309, that he did not realise that the Caledonian and Pictish kingdoms were different, as he makes the former a sub-tribe of the latter. The name Cruithnich is derived, we are told, from the word "cruaidh," which to this day is very frequently used in two senses : first, in that of hardy; and, second, in that of hard-hearted. In both of these it was descriptive of the Cruithnich, as the Irish and Pictish additions to Nennius have it :—

"For plundering known places
And greens without remorse,
For not practising inactivity,
For this they are called Cruithnich."

From the legend as given by the chroniclers we gather that their first settlement in Europe was in Thrace, from whence they passed to France, and from thence to Ireland. On reaching there they found the land occupied by their very kindred race, the Gaidhill, who received them with cordiality, and bestowed lands on them, but on the condition that, as already stated, they would exterminate a British race called the *Sluagh Fea*. The legend gives a wonderful story of the magical arts of this race, in virtue of which any one wounded by them surely died ; and how Drostan, one of the Cruithneachan Druids, completely counteracted this by making the wounded bathe in new milk. The real meaning seems to be that the Sluagh Fea were a wild fierce race, that used poisoned weapons, but for which some great medical priest amongst the Cruithnich found an antidote. The result was that the Sluagh Fea were exterminated, and the Cruithnich settled in Ireland. After this the latter greatly increased in strength; so much so, that Erimon, king of the Gaidhill, asked them to remove to Albin. This they consented to do, and under their king, Cathluan, crossed over to the north of Albin, and, having settled themselves there, proceeded to attack the Britons of the east and south-east, until they drove them southwards, and established a Pictish kingdom from Caithness to the Firth of Forth, extending, in fact, over every part of Albin north of the Forth, except that occupied by the original Gaelic kingdom. We are told that the Cruithnich who established themselves in Albin, being very scarce of women, sent to the Gaidhill of Ireland for wives, their request to a certain extent being granted. This kingdom lasted, as we have already seen, until it was amalgamated with that of the Gaidhill under Kenneth M'Alpin. After this the names Fionn, Scot, and Cruithnich were dropped, and the united Highland races adopted the name of Gaidhill as their common designation. Two hundred years after, in the time of Malcolm Ceanmore, the Court and the Lowlands adopted the names of Scots and Scotland, but the Highlander knows himself only as a Gaidhil.

Such I conceive to be the origin of the Gaidhill,—a race who have carried the fame, the honour, and the industry of their country to the remotest ends of the globe; and whose intensified bravery is written in the history of her battlefields—a race which alas! alas! circumstances are driving from their beloved mountain homes to the lands of the stranger.

The reason of my writing these notes regarding the early history of my native Highlands is, that I find it is being written from a poring over the old chroniclers, and building up therefrom fanciful theories evolved by the writers from their own imaginations. For the explanation of the statements of the old chroniclers, I have, on the other hand, gone to the topographical remains found in the names of places and objects; the monumental, found in old castles, watch-towers, &c.; and the unquestioned traditions as to the names and deeds of our ancestors, which have since infancy been constantly present with me. I claim, therefore, that I have adopted the only system which can give a reasonable foundation for our annals. Amongst these proofs none have been so strangely ignored as those relating to the *Feinne*, and yet none so continually meet us in glen and mountain.

CHAPTER II.

THE CELTIC CHURCH IN THE GAELIC KINGDOM.

THE fact has only of late been popularly realised, that from an early date in the Christian era, onwards until near the time of the Reformation, two churches, differing from each other in essentials, existed side by side in the two ancient kingdoms of Scotland—the *Gaelic* and the *Pictish*. These were the Celtic and the Roman Catholic.

The real distinguishing point, which differentiated the one from the other, was this, that the former was a *non-prelatic* and the latter a *prelatic* church. A church, it must be borne in mind, may be an episcopal without being a prelatic one. The latter holds the doctrine of apostolic succession, with the consequent transmission, through bishops to priests, of supernatural gifts and powers, such as regeneration in baptism, absolution, and others of like kind. The former considers episcopacy to be the best form of church government, and the most conducive to good order and discipline, but repudiates all claims to such miraculous succession, gifts, and powers. It is in the sense thus stated that I use the words *prelacy* and *episcopacy*, and for the clear understanding of what follows it is necessary to lay it down distinctly.

It appears that the earliest Celtic Church consisted of only one order of clergy, it being quite unessential what they were called. This precluded it from being a prelatic church. In a most valuable document of the eighth century, "The Catalogue of the Saints of Ireland according to their different periods," three successional eras in the Irish Celtic Church are described thus:—"The first order of Catholic saints was in the time of Patricius, and then they were all bishops, famous and holy and full of the Holy Ghost; 350 in number, founders of churches. They had one head, Christ; and one chief, Patricius; they observed one mass, one celebration, one tonsure from ear to ear. They celebrated one Easter, on the fourteenth moon after the vernal equinox, and what was excommunicated by one church all excommunicated. They did not reject the society and services of women." Considering that the constitution and government was then tribal and not feudal, the natural inference is, that an ecclesiastic, called in the "Catalogue" a bishop, was appointed to each tribe. This would be about the fifth century. In the next century episcopacy found an entrance, it would seem, for the "Catalogue" says: "The second order was of Catholic presbyters, for in this order there were few bishops but many presbyters. . . . . . They refused the services of women, separating them from the monasteries. This order has hitherto lasted four reigns. They received a mass from Bishops David, Gillas, and Docus, the Britons." After this came a third order "of this sort, they were holy presbyters and a few bishops; one hundred in number, who dwelt in desert places, and lived on herbs and water and the alms." This undoubtedly points to a period when the anchoritical life largely prevailed in the church. Angus the Culdee, in his Litany (ninth century), states that St Patrick ordained seven times fifty bishops with three hundred presbyters. This can be reconciled with the statements in the "Catalogue" by placing it between the first and second order of the latter—that is, betwixt the period when there was only one order of clergy, and that where there were few bishops and many presbyters. Towards the middle of the seventh century episcopacy made a still further, but an exceptional stride towards a higher position. This resulted from Oswald, king of Northumbria, having requested the Celtic Church to send him a bishop. Why he asked for a *bishop*, why the elders of Ii complied with his request, and how they ordained Aidin, the bishop sent him, is fully discussed afterwards. We have no proof whatever, it must be noted, that, although at some periods of her history the Celtic Church permitted a modified and *subjective* episcopacy, she at any time accepted prelacy. Indeed we will see in the sequel that her rule of faith forbade such a supposition.

Before proceeding to show wherein the differences betwixt the two churches consisted, it is necessary to estimate the value of our three leading authorities :—

First. We have Bede's "Ecclesiastical History." Like all the early monkish biographers, he was pitiably facile in believing any amount of fabulous stories illustrative of the miraculous powers of his sainted heroes. He was also a Roman Catholic, and without doubt his views were tinged with the prejudices natural to such a connection. Notwithstanding, his book is invaluable, as what is real can in most cases be distinguished from his fables, and, whilst a sectarian, he is a marvellously honest sectarian.

Second. We have Cummian's "Life of Columba." He succeeded to the abbacy of Ii (corruptly Iona) in the year 657. The life was probably written betwixt 630 and 640. It is written from the Celtic Church point of view, as it should be, and is of great value.

Third. There is Adamnan's "Life of Columba." In this discussion very much depends on the estimate put upon its value. For my own part, I consider that, excepting when he quotes from Cummian,—which he does almost bodily,—that value is of the smallest. It must be noted that he tells us himself that these additions are from tradition and written sources, and the only one of the latter which we know he quotes is Cummian. In the first place, the nature of the additions at once lead to doubt. They consist of ridiculously fabulous stories showing the saint's miraculous powers, and of others tending to show that the Celtic Church held prelacy. As to the first of these, we all know what tradition becomes in the hands of an ecclesiastical admirer writing of the glories of his sainted predecessors. We find Dr Kenedy actually claiming miraculous powers for the Fathers of Ross-shire, and if this is done in the nineteenth century, what would be done in the seventh? As to the second, if it can be shown that Adamnan had an end in view, in which he was intensely interested, and that alterations in such circumstances were not unknown amongst Roman Catholic biographers, a strong case will be made out for the worthlessness of his additions. In order to do so, we must refer to his history. In 679 he became abbat of Ii, and about the year 686 he went on a political mission to his friend Alfrid, king of Northumbria. When there, he was persuaded to forsake the Celtic and join the Roman Church. On his return to Ii he put forth all his strength to induce that community to follow his example, but without success. He then went to Ireland, where his success was much greater, for Bede (b. v. c. xv.) tells that he reduced to "Catholic unity" almost all that "were not under the dominion of Hii," and also "many of the latter." It must be carefully kept in view, that it was not alone, as many would lead us to infer, in the matter of keeping Easter, that Adamnan conformed to the Roman Church, but also, as Bede (b. v. c. xv.) distinctly states, as to "*any other decrees whatsoever.*" After this he paid a visit to Ii, but still without success, and finally left it in 697 for Ireland, where he died in 704. According to some Irish accounts he was expelled from Ii; and it is at the least very likely that he found it too uncomfortable to remain there. It is undoubted that the "Life" was written betwixt his return from England, about 688, and his death. He states that he wrote it at the request of "the brethren," and I think the only reasonable inference is, that by these he meant the many Iian monks in Ireland whom he had persuaded to adopt "Catholic unity." It is most unreasonable to suppose that the monks of Ii itself would ask a renegade from their church, with whom, consequently, they were at bitter variance, to write the life of their founder; whilst, on the other hand, the Irish Iians, who at his bidding had forsaken the Celtic unity, would have a strong motive in asking him to do so, and that in such fashion as would make his great predecessor's beliefs as consonant to those of their adoption as possible. If written in Ireland, the expressions "our monastery," "our island," used by Adamnan, would be appropriate when addressed to Iian monks, although not written in Ii itself. It is quite possible, however, that he may have written it during one of his flying visits to the island. This is of no consequence; what is of consequence is, that it stands to reason that he wrote it at the request of the Iian monks in Ireland. It is, therefore, undoubted that Adamnan had an end to serve, and that one on which he was intensely bent. He could also justify it to himself by the maxim of his church, that this end—the great good of his church—justified the means. That this was not a solitary instance we have a most astounding example of, for we find Jocelyn naively telling us, in his "Life of Kentigern," that he altered the older lives which were his authorities, and which were written from the Celtic point of view, so as to bring them into conformity with "sound doctrine and the Catholic faith." In other words, he plainly tells us that he falsified for the good of his church. In one instance we catch Adamnan in the very act. We find that obsequies in the church of Ii consisted of services of praise in veneration of the departed brother, viz., celebrating the eucharist and chanting (compare Cummian, c. xxiii., with Adamnan, b. iii. c. xxiii. paragraph 10). In relating the obsequies of Columbanus, Cummian says, "Et inter sacra sancti sacrificii mysteria 'hodie ait sanctus' pro s. Columbano episcopo decantandum est;" to this Adamnan deliberately adds *prayers for the dead* (Cummian, c. viii., compared with Adamnan, b. iii. c. xii.). All these things put together: the nature of the additions, the change in Adamnan's faith, his zeal in propagating his new beliefs, the source from which the request came to write the life, the end to be gained, the maxim of his church justifying such tactics, and the exceedingly cognate example in the same or rather in less burning circumstances of Jocelyn, put it, in my opinion, beyond doubt that Adamnan's additions are utterly unreliable and of no value. Further, if so it be, the whole superstructure of prelacy in the Iian Church of Columba's time falls to the ground.

I shall now inquire into what were the differences betwixt the beliefs and usages of the two churches.

1. The Roman Catholic Church held the doctrine of diocesan and prelatic episcopacy. The Celtic Church, as we have seen, at an early date of its history held the very opposite, and had only one order of clergy. At a later date she had an order called bishops, but these were inferior and in entire subjection to the presbyter abbats. Bede says (b. iii. c. iv.): "That island (Ii) has for its ruler an abbat, who is a presbyter, to whose direction all the province, and even the bishops, contrary to the usual method, are subject,

according to the example of their first teacher, who was not a bishop but a presbyter monk." The "Anglo-Saxon Chronicle" (A. 565) thus puts it: "Now in Ii there must ever be an abbat and not a bishop; and all the Scottish bishops ought to be subject to him, because Columba was an abbat and not a bishop."

2. As already seen, the Celtic clergy were allowed to marry. It is true that, during the period of the second order, women were not permitted in the monasteries, as the "Catalogue" puts it, "they refused the services of women, separating them from the monasteries." This was no doubt true of the monastery itself; still it would appear that some connected with them were allowed to marry, as we have in Breadalbane the "Dewars," descended from a "Deoraich," or pilgrim, and also find them in close connection with the monastery of Strathfillan.

3. The Celtic Church had a different tonsure, and kept Easter at a different time from the Roman. These appear to us to be trivial matters; but in these times they formed the subject of the bitterest animosity.

4. The service of baptism and mode of preaching the Word of God were different in the two churches, besides other things not reckoned of so much consequence. Thus we find Augustine (603) saying to the British bishops and others from Bancornburg: "You act in many things contrary to our custom, or rather the custom of the universal church; and yet if you will comply with me in three points, viz., to keep Easter at the due time; to administer baptism, by which we are again born to God, according to custom of the Holy Roman Apostolic Church; and jointly with us to preach the Word of God to the English nation, we will readily tolerate all the other things you do, though contrary to our customs" (Bede, b. ii. c. ii.).

5. By far the most important difference betwixt the two

churches, however, was in the rule of faith; and for this reason, that it guides us to the comprehension of their distinctive standpoints. In cases where the churches leave us in doubt, by omission or indistinctness, as to their tenets, their rule of faith is a sure guide in determining. It is just here that the grand distinction between the two churches comes out. The Roman Church has for its rule of faith the Bible and tradition, and both these infallibly interpreted by the church; the Celtic has for its rule the *Bible alone.* Bede leaves this in no doubt, he says (b. iii. c. iv.): "Wherefore they (the church of Ii) only practised such works of piety and charity as they could learn from the prophetical, evangelical, and apostolical writings." That under works of piety he included ecclesiastical order and ritual, as well as doctrine and life, is manifest from the context, where he had just been referring to the supremacy of the presbyter abbat, and the time of observing Easter—nay, as regards the latter, he gives as the reason for their going by Scripture alone, that they were so far away from the rest of the world that they did not get the synodal decrees. The plain deduction to be made from this celebrated passage is, that the Celtic Church was so completely separated from Rome that it recognised neither its councils or decrees, but walked by the light of Scripture alone. In confirmation of this, Columbanus, as quoted by Mr Skene ("C. S.," p. 104), says the Columban Church "received nought but the doctrine of the evangelists and apostles." Amongst many other difficulties that this fact dispels as to the beliefs of the Celtic Church, it puts an end to all question of its holding prelacy.

Referring to the first of these points of distinction—the supremacy of the presbyter over the bishop,—I must consider a very able argument by Dr Reeves and Mr Skene, to show that, whilst the presbyter possessed the "jurisdiction," the bishop possessed the "function," the former proceeding from "mission," the latter from "orders." A diocesan bishop has jurisdiction, but both agree in saying that there was no diocesan episcopacy in the Celtic Church, and, of course, in this I agree with them. What they mean by "function" is clearly stated by Mr Skene in a foot-note ("C. S.," p. 42) as follows: "by the episcopal functions, as distinguished from diocesan jurisdiction, are meant those ecclesiastical functions appropriated to bishops in virtue of their orders, irrespective of any territorial supervision, such as ordination, confirmation, and celebration of the mass—*pontificali ritu.*" Now it will be noticed that this claims for the bishops of the Celtic Church prelacy, or an inherent power derived from their apostolical succession, to possess themselves and transmit to others sacerdotal powers and supernatural gifts. The only authority given for these momentous claims is two stories from Adamnan (see Adamnan's "Life of Columba" by Reeves, Introduction, pp. cv., cxii., cxiii.; Skene, "C. S.," pp. 94, 95; and Adamnan, b. i. c. xxix. and xxxv.). These, however, are taken from the additions made to Cummian by Adamnan, and having already shown, as I believe I have done, that these are utterly unreliable, the argument completely fails. It would be easy indeed to show that, even although more reliable than they are, they are easily explained by the transmutation of tradition passing through favouring hands; but the worthlessness of Adamnan's additions, from which they come, renders this unnecessary. I speak with the highest respect of Dr Reeves and Mr Skene, to whose researches and facts every student of Celtic Church history must feel unbounded obligations; but this respect, great as it is, cannot prevent my stating, as plainly as I can, where I differ from their conclusions.

I must, however, before leaving the subject, express great

28   *The Celtic Church in the Gaelic Kingdom.*

doubts as to whether there was such an official as a bishop at all connected with the community at Ii at so early a date as that of Columba. We have no direct proof that there was, and can only infer it from there being without doubt bishops in some of the Irish monasteries. There is one consideration, however, of extreme consequence in this last connection which has been lost sight of, and that is, that there were a few monasteries in Ireland, founded by students of the Roman Catholic school at Whithorn, and that in these bishops and not presbyters presided. It is a great mistake to apply the ecclesiastical order in these to Celtic foundations. Dr Reeves commits this serious error (Adamnan, Introduction, p. cv.) when he says, in reference to *an assumed* disclamation by Columba of equality with episcopal rank, " This was no more than was to be expected from a presbyter who had served as a deacon in a monastery where presbyters, called from their chief function *ministri altaris,* lived under the presidency of a bishop." The monastery here referred to is Moyville, which was an offshoot of Whithorn. It is true that Columba in his youth resided there for some time, but it is just as true that he left it and joined a Celtic Church monastery, whose order, discipline, and doctrine he adopted. It is inadmissible to say, as Dr Reeves does, that in founding a monastery of his own Columba "was to be expected" to adopt a system which he had deliberately and finally rejected. Further, when Aidin was appointed bishop to the Northumbrians, he was selected and ordained as such by the Celtic Church elders or presbytery. In doing so they only did what the Alexandrian Church was wont to do prior to the year 246 ; for, as Jerome tells us in his letter to Evagrius, the presbyters in that church " unum ex selectum in excelsiori gradu collocatum episcopum nominabant." I refer more fully to the Irish Roman Catholic monasteries and the ordination of Aidin afterwards. It is sufficient in the meantime to say, that the latter shows that episcopal ordination was not the rule of the Scottish Celtic Church of the early part of the seventh century.

I now go on to give a general view of the history of the Celtic Church, leaving those interested to fill up the outline.

There is no doubt as to the time when Roman Catholicism was introduced into Albin. This took place at the very close of the fourth century, when St Ninian founded the church at Whithorn amidst the Pictish colony of Galloway. He also extended his mission to the Picts, occupying the eastern portion of the kingdom, situated to the north of the Forth. That he was successful may be with certainty inferred from the fact, that the Roman Church ever afterwards held a firm footing there, and, as we will afterwards see, during one century had a complete ascendancy.

There are different theories as to the origin of the Celtic Church in Scotland. One is that St Ninian and St Patrick founded it in Ireland, from whence it passed into the Gaelic kingdom of Scotland. Another has it that it existed in the latter from a much earlier period, and came not from Ireland but from South Britain. With this latter I agree.

We really don't know much of St Patrick; what we do know is chiefly from two writings of his, supposed to be genuine—his "Confession" and his "Letter to Coroticus." We have two incidental notices of him, one by Cummian and one by Adamnan; but it is an unaccountable fact, if, as later authors assert, Ireland was converted by him, that not one single writer for more than four hundred years after his death made any mention of it. It is utterly inconceivable that Bede, if such was the case, would have passed over it in silence. Besides, his own writings, already referred to, bear evidence that any success he had was not permanent. If Ninian actually went to Ireland, he must have been equally unsuccessful. There is one fact which proves this. Both Patrick and Ninian were Roman Catholics, and if Christianity and its offshoot, the Celtic Church, were there founded by them, then their church must have been of the same type as the Roman. We have, however, already seen that the very reverse was the case, and that on its coming into the light of day, especially in the sixth century, it not only differed, but radically differed from the Roman Church. For the first century and a half or two centuries of its existence the Roman Church shows some similarity of type to that afterwards exhibited in the Celtic; but subsequently, that is to say after the development in it of prelatic dogmatism, the types are fundamentally opposed to each other. It has also been suggested that the failure of Patrick in Ireland was in some measure due to the tribal system then prevailing, and which tended, from its great parity in rank amongst all the members, in another direction than that of a hierarchy. This, however, cannot account for it, as we have found that St Ninian in similar circumstances succeeded amongst the Pictish tribes of Scotland.

The inevitable conclusion is, that the Celtic Church, being of an entirely different stamp from the Roman Catholic, arose at an earlier date than that of Patrick and Ninian, and that the missions of these for the purpose of conforming it to the latter were grievous failures.

The question now comes, Have we any proof that Christianity reached Britain at an earlier date? Undoubtedly we have. An ancient chronicler of Dover Castle, quoted by Dugdale in his account of St Martin's Nunnery, says, "In the year of grace 180 reigned in Britain, Lucius. He became a Christian under Pope Eleutherius, and served God and advanced Holy Church as much as he could." Bede and the "Saxon Chronicle" confirm this, although with some variation in the chronology. Tertullian, writing about the beginning of the third century, confirms the fact that at this time Britain had received the faith of Christ. In the persecution by Diocletian, about the beginning of the fourth century, we find that there was not only a church in Britain, but that Alban and others suffered martyrdom. British ecclesiastics were present at the first Council of Arles in 314, and asserted opinions differing from those of Rome. We have the testimony of Chrysostom, and other circumstances later. If, therefore, Christianity had obtained a footing in Britain during the second and third centuries, we can have no difficulty in believing that it extended to the Gaelic kingdoms of Scotland and Ireland. In Buchanan* (Aikman's Ed. vol. i. p. 199) we have the following: "Freed from external cares, the Scots now chiefly exerted themselves for the promotion of the Christian religion, to which they were incited by the following occurrence: Multitudes of the Britons, fearing the cruelty of Diocletian to the Christians, sought refuge among them, of whom many illustrious for the purity of their doctrine and the uprightness of their lives remained in Scotland, &c." It would appear from this that, even before this time, Christianity had reached the Gaelic kingdom; but, in any case, its propagation by those fleeing from the Diocletian persecution bears on the face of it extreme probability. From the close intercourse of the two Gaelic kingdoms of Ireland and Scotland, there can be small doubt if it got a footing in one it would do so in the other.

* To prevent all misconception as to the weight I place on so modern a historian as Buchanan, I cite him simply to show that the tradition, written or unwritten, from which he quoted three centuries ago, is to the same effect as that which, from other sources, we have yet.

The next great era in the history of the Celtic Church is a notable one. It occurred about the beginning of the sixth century, and consisted of that most glorious revival of religious life which, like a mighty wave, swept first over Ireland and then over Scotland, carrying its effects far into the continent of Europe. The external cause of this great impulse seems to have been a startling development of monastic and anchoritic life. Men, some of noble and even royal birth, and equally noble and royal character, others, if not so high in rank, yet equally high in all the qualities that rendered them ablest and foremost in this mighty battle of Christ against ignorance and sin, felt themselves constrained by a mighty power which they could not repress, to go down where the battle was hottest, and there to quit them as giants in the fight. Leaving all the joys and happinesses of family life, subjecting themselves to privations, painful wanderings, sore trials, and even to death itself, they devoted themselves to proclaiming the eternal blessedness of unwavering faith in that risen and glorified Redeemer who can save even the chief of sinners. It is true that, as a rule, such departures from God's ordination of the family life, as the monastic and anchoritic, are fraught with far more evil than good; but who dare say but there are mighty crises when such exceptional devotion calls down an unspeakable blessing. It is indeed a great sight that sweeps across our mental vision, as we call up small companies of men, with staves in their hands, and clad in long woollen robes, their zeal intensifying with their mission, showing itself in every lineament of their countenances, beaming in every glance of their eyes, lighted up as these glances were by the burning enthusiasm glowing in their earnest spirits; and ever as they went along proclaiming the glad tidings that were saturating themselves with peace and joy, and filling up the noblest and highest aspirations of their spiritual being. This intense impulse seems to have reached the Celtic Church of Ireland, from the British Church of Wales, a church of the most kindred form and spirit.

In order, however, to read correctly the history of the Celtic Church at this time, it must, as already adverted to, be carefully borne in mind that there were a few other monasteries in Ireland of quite a different type. These received their inspiration either from Whithorn or some other Roman Catholic source, and were governed in entire subjection to the doctrine, order, and discipline of that church. The monastery of Moyville has been already referred to as one of these. Its founder was Finnian or Findbar, and in it Columba spent part of his early years. We may also instance the monasteries of Clones and Ardshaws, their respective founders being Tighernac and Eugenius, who were carried away in their boyhood from Ireland by pirates, and brought to Scotland, where they were sent for instruction to Whithorn. On arriving at manhood, they returned to their native country, and founded these monasteries, adopting, of course, the system under which they had been reared. In this class of monastery, as we find in the case of Moyville,* and by inference in the others, there were three orders of clergy, bishops, ministers, and deacons, whilst the head of the community was not an abbat but a bishop. This was in perfect contrariety to the usages of the Celtic Church, and when its system is endeavoured to be explained by the customs of quite a different church, an utterly mistaken view is given of it. We can only get at correctness by comparing for inference Celtic monasteries with Celtic, and Roman with Roman. By neglect of this unquestionable criterion, Dr Reeves has in some instances given very distorted delineations of the usages and beliefs of the former.

* Cummian, c. iv.

Columba having left the Roman Church monastery of Moyville, joined the Celtic Church monastery of Clonards, presided over at that time by another Finnian. The system of this latter he adopted, and unbendingly held to the end of his life. In the year A.D. 563, he came to Ii and founded there his celebrated monastery. It was in constitution purely Celtic. Columba governed not only this, his own special monastery, but also all the other Celtic monasteries in Scotland with undisputed sway. We have no proof that there was such a thing then as a bishop at Ii, and I question, from the temperament of the man, if he would have suffered the interference of such an official, whether "jurisdictional" or "functional." Kings, princes, nobles, and the pious of many lands flocked to this monastery for instruction and Christian fellowship, whilst its mighty influence is still felt in the land. Columba found Christianity existing in the Gaelic and Pictish kingdoms, but to him remained the privilege of converting from Druidism the northern Picts. He died A.D. 597, full of veneration and honour.

The next event of moment in the history of the Scottish Celtic Church demanding attention was the sending of missionaries to Northumbria. Oswald having succeeded to the Northumbrian throne, "sent to the elders of the Scots, among whom he and his followers, when in banishment, had received the sacrament of baptism, desiring they would send him a bishop, by whose instruction and ministry the English nation which he governed might be taught the advantages and receive the sacraments of the Christian faith" (Bede b. iii. c. iii.). In the first place they sent him a presbyter, a man of severe temperament, and who utterly failed in his mission. On his return he reported to an assembly of the elders his want of success. "Then, said Aidian, who was also present in the council, to the presbyter then spoken of, 'I am of opinion, brother, that you were more severe to your unlearned hearers than you ought to have been, and did not at first, conformably to the apostolic rule, give them the milk of more easy doctrine, till by degrees, nourished with the Word of God, they should be capable of greater perfection, and be able to practise God's sublime precepts.' Having heard these words, all present began diligently to weigh what he had said, and presently concluded that he deserved to be made a bishop, and ought to be sent to instruct the incredulous and unlearned, since he was found to be endued with singular discretion, which is the mother of other virtues, and accordingly being ordained, they sent him to their friend King Oswald" (Bede b. iii. c. v.). This would be about the year 634. It will be noticed that the plain inference to be drawn is, that he was ordained by the elders. There is not one word of the ordination being by other bishops, or even of a bishop having been present. The after refusal of the Roman Church to acknowledge as valid the ordination of British or Celtic bishops (Bede b. iii. c. xxviii.), goes in further proof of this. Why Oswald asked for a *bishop* is not said, but it is a very natural inference that he did so for the sake of expediency. The Northumbrians, although at this time fallen away from the faith, had shortly before embraced the Roman Catholic form of Christianity through the preaching of Paulinus, and were then accustomed to the hierarchy and gorgeous rites of that church. They were also in Oswald's time brought into contact with nations, amongst whom this external splendour in ecclesiastical usage prevailed. Knowing, therefore, the influence which outward pomp on the one hand, and supernatural assumptions on the other, has always exercised over the half-cultured, Oswald may have thought that the services of a bishop, albeit a Celtic one, would be more imposing and successful than those of a presbyter; and the elders of Ii for the same reason, although contrary to their custom, may have gratified him in this matter. They may have the more readily done so as their first missionary, a presbyter, failed. Other bishops of the same kind were afterwards sent, and some things which they did, such as consecrating other bishops single-handed, must appear strange to prelatists. The matter at last came to a point, for, as Bede tells us, there being no canonically ordained bishops in all Britain but one, Wini, a Roman Catholic,—British and Celtic bishops not counting as such,—two of these uncanonical British bishops were called in with Wini to ordain Chad bishop of York (Bede b. iii. c. xxviii.). This, however, was too much for Theodore, archbishop of Canterbury, who in bitter terms expressed his contempt for such claims to bishopdom, and had Chad reconsecrated after the Catholic manner, which no doubt meant by three Roman Catholic prelates. This mission only lasted for about thirty years, Northumbria having then returned to Roman Catholicism. Colman, the then Celtic bishop, with many others, refusing to conform, returned to Scotland, whilst Ceode, Chad, and others conformed and remained in England. In fact, this Celtic bishopism in England seems to have been factitious, and soon collapsed.

During the seventh century the Celtic Church of Ii appears to have spread not only over the northern, but also over part of the eastern Pictish kingdom, but in these a great reverse came over it early in the eight century, in consequence of Naitan, the Pictish king, joining the Roman Church. In 710 he issued decrees compelling all his nation to follow his example, and as the Celtic clergy proved recalcitrant, in 717 he expelled them from his dominions. They only recovered their freedom in Pictland at the accession of Kenneth M'Alpin to the joint sovereignty of both nations—the Picts and Scots—in 836. The flourishing period of the Iian monastery extended from Columba's arrival in 563, to Adamnan's return from England in 688.

The discord he introduced in attempting to bring in the Roman Catholic rites completely destroyed its peace, and its further declension was accomplished by Naitan's ejection of the Celtic Church clergy. After that, its influence greatly diminished, until the ravages of the Northmen necessitated the removal of Columba's remains to Ireland, and the transference of the chief seat of Scottish Celtic worship to Dunkeld.

We now reach that disastrous epoch in the history of the Celtic Church, when Malcolm Ceanmore in the eleventh century married Margaret of England. Ancient and modern writers combine in extolling the virtues and piety of this queen. I believe that she was sincere, but it was with the sincerity of those pharisees who would compass sea and land to make a proselyte, or of Paul in those days when he thought he was doing God service by persecuting the church of Christ. She was the quintessence of sectarian bigotry. Her piety was of that sickliest, and, when combined with power, most dangerous kind, which believes the voice of the priest to be the voice of God. It is this sort of piety, if such it can be called, which has lighted the fires of persecution, and deluged the earth with the blood of the martyrs. Malcolm in ecclesiastical matters was entirely led by her, and she in her turn by her confessor Turgot and other priests. He was so superstitious and ignorant, that he would take her books turned upside down into his hands and piously kiss them, as if they were a fetish. The result was that the Celtic Church was in every way trodden upon, and superseded by the English Roman Catholic. This persecution and supercession was continued by their successors, especially by David I. of priest worshipping memory, who amongst much else of the same kind expelled the old Culdean monks from their foundations, and supplied their places by Benedictines and Augustinians. Well does Buchanan say, "the name (Culdees) and the institution remained until a more recent kind of monks, divided into a number of orders, expelled them, which latter were as much their inferiors in doctrine and piety, as their superiors in riches, ceremonies, and other external rites by which the eye is captivated and the mind deceived." Although thus externally superseded, the teachings of the ancient church were not lost, but remained imbedded in the minds and hearts of the Gaidhill. In this way we can account for the rapid progress of the reformed doctrines in many parts of the Gaelic kingdom, and especially in Breadalbane, Glenlyon, and Fortingall. It is a strange fact, how many of the customs and beliefs peculiar to the Druidic worship have remained in a lingering fashion amongst us, and that conjoined with an extreme Presbyterianism, whilst those peculiar to the Roman Catholic Church have almost entirely perished. I well remember an incident of my boyhood, when my old nurse, one of the sternest of Calvinists, directed me in the event of a stone being under my foot when I got the first glimpse of a new moon, to take it up and treasure it as a sort of talisman.

In these notes on the Celtic Church, and what follows, I don't profess to have reached that sublime atmosphere above the clouds, where all swayings by ecclesiastical surroundings are unknown, simply because I believe such to be impossible, and that professions of that kind only lead to extreme suspicion of real one-sidedness, invariably justified. I have, however, endeavoured to put forth no statement of fact but what has all the foundation I claim for it, whether that be actual or referential. I hope I have not said one word to hurt the feelings of Roman Catholics, some of whom have been my kind friends and honoured acquaintances. They believe in a *jure divino* prelacy. I believe in no *jure divino*, either Prelatic or Presbyterian. We both hold loyally to our opinions and respect each other accordingly. I will go further and say, that whilst I can understand a *non jure divino* Episcopalian not being a Roman Catholic, I cannot understand any one believing in a *jure divino* as inherent in either a priest or bishop being other than a Roman Catholic. I believe this to have been the radical difference betwixt the Celtic and the Roman Catholic Church, and that if the former believed in a "functional" episcopacy, which is only another name for prelacy, it need not have made such a bitter fight against conforming to the latter.

CHAPTER III.

MONASTERY OF II AND ST COLUMBA.

COLUMBA having sailed from Ireland about the year 563, with twelve companions, came to the island Ii, situated to the south-west of Mull, and from which it is separated by a narrow sound. Having received a gift of the island from the Picts, or from the Scots and Picts jointly, he established on it that monastery whose history makes such a notable landmark in the religious annals of Scotland, and especially in those of the Gaidhiltachd or Gaelic kingdom. It was entirely a community of monks, no women being allowed on the island. They were divided into classes—one for out-door, another for in-door work, and a third for all the duties connected with the performance of worship. Amongst the working class were those we would now call tradesmen—such as carpenters, smiths, boat-builders, and others. The duties attendant on public worship were probably in charge of the seniors, and the most eminent amongst whom also, were those employed in making copies of the Scriptures. Besides the services of public worship, some at least of the monks were in the habit of occasionally retiring to secluded places for exercises—such as prayer, reading, contemplation, and reciting portions of the Bible. The place is still pointed out on Weem Rock, in Perthshire, where St Cuthbert sat for whole nights, immersed to the middle in cold water, reciting the Psalter. There were different functionaries connected with these Celtic monasteries, and with Ii in particular, which demand mention.

1. *Bishops.*—Of these I have already spoken. It is very doubtful if there were such at all at Ii in Columba's time. Afterwards there were, but, as I have shown, they were entirely inferior and subject to the presbyter who was abbat.

2. *The Scribe or Writing-Master.*—The copying of the Scriptures or part of the Scriptures was quite an institution in the Celtic monasteries—Columba himself was an eminent transcriber. Manuscripts, ornamented and illuminated, have come down to us of very great beauty, and bearing a characteristic impress peculiar to the Celtic Church. As few of the laity could read or write, it was a matter of vital necessity to the success of the missions that copies of the Bible should be in every church and in the possession of every missionary for reading to the people. We have already seen that the teaching of the Celtic Church was entirely based on Scripture. The office, therefore, of scribe to the monastery was a most important and respected one.

3. *Ferleighinn or Reader.*—We find that whenever the monks were gathered together, either at meal times or after the day's work was ended, suitable books, such as the lives of the Saints, were read to them. Consequently there arose the requirement of a reader to the community. Such a functionary is not mentioned in the lives of Columba, but afterwards appears in connection with some of the monasteries. It may have been in existence at the earlier period although not mentioned.

4. We find two orders of anchorites connected with the monasteries who were not resident, but who could at any time be recalled to assume office or otherwise. Of these

the one went by the name of *Deorich* or *Dewars*, the other by that of *Cuiltich* or *Culdees*.

The Deorich were wandering anchorites or solitaries who devoted themselves to God and austerities, and who, as they passed from place to place, built themselves temporary cells in retired situations. Bede* speaks of one Wictbert, who, towards the end of the seventh century, "had lived many years a stranger (or wanderer, *peregrinus*) in Ireland, leading an anchoritical life in great purity." In the charters of the Columban house of Kells,† conferring lands upon Deorich, it is said, " Ro edpairset didu na huli sin Diseart Cholumchille hi' Cennanus cona Luibgortan do Dia ocus do Deoradaib craibdechait do gres cen sheilbs ndilis do nach erraid ann treun buithu co ro chinne a bethaid do Dia ocus corp craidbech," the translation of which appears to me to be, " For imparting to them the whole Diseart of Cholumchille in Kells, together with the enclosed loop of land, to God, and to Deorich given up to austerities, for the purpose of giving possession therein to every wanderer faithful with all his powers, and for his whole life to God, and to a body devoted to austerities." One thing is certain from this extract, that an anchoritic Deoraich is also styled a *wanderer* devoted to God and to austerities. It also throws light upon the word *peregrinus* in Bede, which evidently means the very same kind of anchoritic life as Deoraich or Erraid does in the charter, and therefore should be translated " wandering anchorite." It appears also from this extract that the anchoritic vows of the Deoraich did not necessarily extend to his whole lifetime, as the very providing of a shelter for those of them who became devoted for life, shows that the vows of others were temporary, when they probably returned to family life. Thus, as before stated, we

* B. iv. c. ix.
† Quoted by Dr Reeves, "Life of Adamnan," p. 125.

have in Breadalbane the well-known family of "Deorich-na-faraichd" or "Dewars of the Crozier," who are evidently the descendants of some notable Deoraich. The name probably comes from *diobarach*, a wanderer, or from *diobaraoraich*, a wandering worshipper. The following from the lament for Clann Uisnich shows the meaning attached to the word—

> " Codal uile's beag a lochd,
> Do dhaoine bhiodh ri *deoireachd;*
> Ge d'nach biodh coga fo na ghrein
> Ach daoine bhi as an tir fein."

> " Sleep is altogether momentary to men who are at *wanderings;*
> Even if there be no such thing as war under the sun,
> Yet if men are away from their own country." *

Judging from the statement as to the third order of saints in the Irish Catalogue, we may conclude that the Deorich existed as early as the end of the sixth century.

The other class of non-resident anchorites, who were called *Cuiltich* or *Cuildich* in contradistinction to the Deorich or wanderers, took up their abode in one place, where they continued to reside unless recalled to their parent monastery. They take their name from *cuile*, a word signifying a recess or retired place. Cuiltich therefore means the men of the recess or retreat. *Cuile* in this connection is applied in three different ways—

First. It is the old Gaelic name for a church. Buchanan refers this signification to a very early date. After stating that many Britons, illustrious for their piety, sought refuge among the Scots from the Diocletian persecution, he says that they "led a solitary life, with such a reputation for sanctity among all ranks, that upon their decease, the cells they inhabited were changed into churches, and from that

* See Gillies's "Dain agus Orain Gaidhealach," 1786, p. 260.

custom it still continues that the ancient Scots call churches cells. This species of religious they called Culdees." This statement of the historian is in accordance with the tradition of the kingdom. There can be no doubt that the word here translated cell, was originally the Gaelic *cuile*, or in Irish *chilla* or *g'ceall*.* It has now passed into *Kil*,† and is used in multiplied instances to signify a church, as Kilmarnock, Kilbride, Kilmory, and many others.

Second. This word cuile is also applied to a hut erected near a monastery, where any of the monks, at least those under monastic vows, could temporarily retire for religious exercises. This I conceive is the meaning of the word *chill* or *g'ceall* in Columba's name, and not church as many suppose. The "Leabar Breac" says that he got this designation in consequence of the frequency with which he came to meet the neighbouring children, from the *chill* where he read his psalms; whilst the children would say amongst themselves, "In tanic ar Colum Beeni indui on chill"— "Has our little Callum come to-day from the Chill." ‡ Bede says, "he is now by some called Columb-kill, the name being compounded from Columb and cell." It may mean church, as the word is really the same, but I think the other is by far the most likely. This view of it is further confirmed by his having at Ii a hut or retreat called in Latin tugurium, tuguriolum, and hospitium, which he used not only as a dormitory, but also for transcribing the Psalter in, and for purposes of devotion and of communion with God.§ In the particulars of St Faolan's life, given in the "Breviary

---

* *See* Appendix iii.

† This prefix must be distinguished from another, the modern spelling of which is the same, viz., *cille*, a burying-ground, and which is found in some names such as Killin.

‡ B. iv. c. ix.

§ Adamnan, b. iii. c. xxiii., xxiv. ; also Cummian.

of Aberdeen" we have the following :—" In this monastery
(St Mund's), that he might the more easily labour in divine
contemplation, he secretly constructed a cell not far from
the cloister." Chad had a dwelling of a similar kind at the
Abbey of Lestingau, and Aengus, called the *Culdee*, the
author of the well-known Litany, built a *cuile* for himself
near the monastery of Clonenaugh."* We also find at Ii a
building called *Cothan cuildich*, and interpreted in the old
"Statistical Account" to mean "Culdee's cell" or "couch."
All these show that such cells or cuiltean were usually near
monasteries. They were probably confined to those monks
who had taken on them either permanent or temporary
eremitical vows.

Third. The word cuile is further applied to the hut of
a cuilteach or culdee who lived away from the monastery.
It was usually built of wattles faced with earth or sods and
thatched. It contained two apartments, an outer for the
ordinary purposes of life, and an inner for the performance
of religious services. Cuilteach means the man of the
cuile. Occasionally a cuilteach set up his hut by himself
alone, in a solitary place ; such was Beccan the Solitary, to
whom, along with Segine of Ii, Cummian of Ireland
addressed his letter of 634. Usually, however, a number
of cuiltich associated themselves together and erected their
cuiltean at one place, and which was called a diseart.
They did not live as a community, but separately and independently, each having his own hut and food, and following
such rules for his private work and worship as he saw fit.
For public worship they met at the common cuile or church,
and besides there seems to have been a common official,
styled a *Ceann-diseart*, whose duties are not mentioned, but
who probably exercised such control in their external affairs
as prevented friction either amongst themselves or with

* Joyce's "Irish Names of Places," 1st series, p. 158.

their neighbours. Their food consisted of such fruits, grain, and vegetables as they could rear, along with the gifts of the people, which would then be chiefly not in money but in kind. We have good grounds for believing that this class of religious had a very early origin in the Gaidhiltachd. We have already seen that Buchanan refers to them as existing in the Gaelic kingdom in the time of Diocletian, if not earlier. Joscelyn in his "Life of Kentigern," no doubt quoting from the earlier lives, refers to them as existing in the sixth century; and although, as I have already shown, both he and Adamnan are utterly untrustworthy where matters of faith and doctrine are concerned, yet in simple matters of fact, having no such concern, they may be trusted. He tells us that the mature disciples of Kentigern "dwelt, as did Kentigern himself, in single cottages. . . . Therefore these solitary clerics were called in common speech Calledei." Dr Jamieson reports the tradition of the Gaidhiltachd truly when he says, "There is, I am informed, a pretty general tradition in the Highlands of Scotland that the Culdees immediately succeeded the Druids as the ministers of religion, and it is said that they received the name of Cuildeach, as delighting, like the priests of heathenism, in retired situations." It would appear from the "Catalogue of the Saints," that the eremitical life did not fully take root in Ireland until the sixth century, but the tradition of the Gaelic kingdom is entirely confirmatory of the statements of Buchanan and Dr Jamieson, that the Cultich had in it a much earlier origin, stretching back, as the latter has it, to the emergence from Druidism. Indeed, the word was applied to the retreats or groves of the Druids, as it is noteworthy in reference to the tradition of their seeking, like these priests of heathenism, retired situations, that cuile means not only a retreat consisting of a hut or building, but is very often applied to a recess in a glen or wood. The cuile may not, therefore, have been in all cases an erection of any kind, but simply a place situated apart. We have an instance of Columba himself seeking such a place on the western plain of Ii.* Putting all these things together, I scarcely think that any Gaidhil who knows the traditions of his kingdom, its language, and its usages, will for a moment doubt of the existence of the Cuiltich at a very early period.

It is, however, a very different question, when the translation of Cuiltich into Latin, as Kaledei or Calledei came into use. The English word Culdee evidently is a translation from the Latin, and must of course have had a still later origin. We find the word Calledei neither in Bede nor in the biographies of Columba. The order itself is plainly enough referred to, although not by that name. Bede for instance refers† to Fursey, Ultan, Ethelwald, and others; and the biographers of Columba to Finan of Durrow and Fergna of Muirbulcmar, who were clearly Cuiltich.‡ We have besides in the life of Columba, several references to parties who went forth in search of Disearts. It would appear therefore, that the term Calledei, which is the Latin translation of the old Gaelic word Cultich, and Culdee the English translation of the Latin, did not come at least into general use until after Adamnan and Bede. Other derivations of Calledei have been given besides the traditional one. Dr Reeves takes it from *Gille-Dhe*, or servant of God. I am not aware, however, of any authority whatever, historical or traditional, for this derivation. Individuals, however, got this appellation; for instance it is very probable that Angus, the author of the Litany, was so designated. In like manner we find *Gille-Christ*, servant of Christ, from one of whom so called comes the Macgilchrists; *Gille-Faolan*, servant of Faolan,

---

* Adamnan, b. iii. c. xvii.   † *Ibid.* b. iii. c. xviii.; v. c. i.
‡ Adamnan, b. i. 34, and iii. 24.

from whom the Maclellans, and many others. These, however, were individual and not class appellations. Besides, it appears to me as if Dr Reeves's Gille-Dhe was a translation into Gaelic of the English Culdee, and not, as it should be, a translation of the Gaelic Cuiltich into the English. I agree with Mr Skene when he makes Culdees to be a translation of Calledei, but entirely differ when he makes the latter to be an inversion of Deicolæ. It is much too violent, and as far as I know, without example. The only one given, that of Christicolæ into the Irish Celechrist, is not apposite, as this term is the same that is above referred to, and is applied at least in the Scottish kingdom to individuals and not classes. But independently, however, of this argument, such a derivation is not only without warrant from Scottish history or tradition, but completely sets aside the whole lingual and traditional history of the kingdom.

The founder and first abbot of Ii was Columba. There are two men—Columba and Knox—who, above all others, have left their mark on the Christianity of Scotland; and I cannot help thinking that there are strong points of resemblance betwixt them. They were both possessed of utter fearlessness, perfect disregard of consequences when in the path of duty, stern determination of will, indomitable perseverance, and an imperious temper. It is doubtful, indeed, if without these characteristics in a greater or less degree, any have become giants amongst their fellows, so as to leave behind them their indelible foot-prints on the annals of the social and spiritual life and history of their nations. In judging of such men, it must be borne in mind that grace does not change the natural temperament, it only purifies it and diverts its streams into a different channel, and towards a different end and object. Often and often do some of its waters flow back into the old groove, causing that fearful conflict betwixt flesh and spirit which made even an apostle exclaim "who will deliver me," but in which the final victory is certain. Without having this full in view we never can estimate aright the lives of such men as David, Peter, Paul, Columba, or Knox. By natural temperament Columba was haughty, imperious, and proud. An unprejudiced reading of his history leaves the full impression that family or personal pride, or perhaps both combined, made him a powerful integer in bringing about the bloody war which ended with the battle of Cul-Dreimhne; and that his own deep contrition for his share in it, along probably with the censure of his church, caused him to leave Ireland. Taking therefore his twelve companions with him, he left his native country, and sailed across to Ii, of which he received possession, and where he immediately set about establishing that notable monastery, to which in due time flocked kings, princes, nobles, and the pious of every land; and in which they received culture, learning, zeal for God's cause, and the pure truths of an uncontaminated Bible. Over this and all the other Celtic monasteries scattered throughout the Gaelic kingdom and northern Pictland, Columba as presbyter-abbat ruled supreme. He selected and within its walls ordained Aidin as king of the Gaidhil-tachd; and whilst thus exercising immense influence in Scotland, he still retained no mean sway in many parts of Ireland. In his own monastery, work, hospitality, fasting, censure, the order of public worship, and the preaching of the Word in its purity, were entirely under his control. On coming to Scotland he found Christianity already existing in the Gaelic kingdom, but the whole of northern Pictland still under the reign of Druidism. With characteristic vigour, he set about intensifying religion in the one, and introducing it into the other kingdom. For the former purpose he established monasteries, and for the latter he passed on to Inverness, and gained over Brude, the Pictish king, to the true faith. From thence he made his way to the other towns and villages, until the whole nation received the gospel.

From the many incidents related of him, we can picture to our mind's eye, a man, small in stature, but of graceful and eloquent speech, clad in a white tunic, and long hooded over-robe of woollen cloth, sandals on his feet, and a crooked staff in his hand. At one time receiving and consecrating a king; at another tenderly consoling some trembling penitent, or compassionately caring for the welfare of a solitary crane that had wandered away from his native land. Again the scene changes, and we see him now passing through the fields superintending the work, and encouraging the workmen; anon in his cell transcribing the Psalter, or holding fellowship with God; and then passing to the sea-shore to receive some coming stranger, and afterwards entertaining him with the genuine hospitality and true-bred courtesy of the Highland gentleman. In the church we picture him with loving zeal arranging and directing the order of service, and joining therein with glowing joy and fervour. We almost fancy we hear that wonderful voice, which, in chanting the Psalter, seemed to those near him to be mellowed into the softest beauty, whilst those at a mile's distance heard with vivid distinctness and thrilling power every word that he uttered. Such is the exquisite vision that passes athwart our mind's eye, as with earnest gaze we contemplate the daily life of Columba.

We are told that "he was beloved by all;* for a holy joy ever beaming on his face revealed the joy and gladness with which the holy spirit filled his inmost soul." But here, in arriving at his true character, we must discriminate. The love he called forth was not that softly affectionate passion, which as it were unawares clings with tenderest filaments, and wraps itself with constant and absorbing tenderness round some beloved object. No! the nature

* Adamnan's Second Preface.

of the man, and the high exercises of his spiritual being, forbade this. His far-off reserve and his self-absorbed communings with his God and Saviour, communings which made even his countenance to beam with heavenly joy, awakened a love in those who intimately approached him, wherein awe combined with reverence and even trembling largely mingled. There was one exception, however — Diormit, his constant companion and faithful servant — who loved him with the most childlike and engrossing love. That this love was reciprocated we know, for laying to one side the miracle-mongering of his later biographer, it yet remains that during an illness of Diormit's, seemingly unto death, Columba was intensely affected, and with all the fervour of his spirit entreated God for his recovery.

On the last day of his life he went forth accompanied by Diormit to bless the barn. On entering it he blessed the heaps of winnowed corn, and gave expression to his thanks in these words, "I heartily congratulate my beloved monks, that this year also, if I am obliged to depart from you, you will have a sufficient supply." Diormit on hearing this began to feel sad, and remonstrated, saying, "this year, at this time, father, thou very often vexest us, by so frequently making mention of thy leaving us." Whereupon the saint revealed to him that that same night "at midnight, which commenceth the solemn Lord's day, I shall, according to the sayings of Scripture, go the way of our fathers. For already my Lord Jesus Christ deigneth to invite me, and to Him I say, in the middle of the night shall I depart at His invitation." Diormit hearing these words wept bitterly, and the saint with all tenderness endeavoured to console him. He then ascended the hill over-looking the monastery, and having stood for a little time on its summit, he uplifted both his hands and blessed it, saying, "small and mean though this place is, yet shall it be held in great and unusual honour, not only by Scotic kings and people, but also by the rulers of foreign and barbarous nations, and by their subjects; the saints also even of other churches shall regard it with no common reverence." Returning to his cell, he sat transcribing the Psalter until he came to that verse of the 33d Psalm, where it is written, "They that seek the Lord shall want no manner of thing that is good." "Here," said he "at the end of the page I must stop, and what follows let Baithene write." He then went to church for the evening service, and as soon as this was over he returned to his chamber and spent the remainder of the night in bed, having a bare flag for his couch and for his pillow a stone. As soon as the midnight bell tolled, he rose hastily and went to the church. Diormit following him cried out "Where art thou, father?" and groping in the darkness found him lying before the altar, raised him up a little and placed his head on his bosom. Meanwhile the other monks running in with their lights burst into lamentations. Diormit raised the saint's right hand that he might bless them. Having done so by feebly moving his fingers, he immediately breathed his last.

There was a strange similarity, as in the life so in the death, of the two great Christian teachers of Scotland. John Knox lay speechless when his faithful Bannatyne asked him to give them a sign that he died in perfect trust. Upon this he lifted up one of his hands, and sighing twice, expired without a struggle.

So died, indicating their stedfast and abiding faith, those two men who, in the conflict of truth and righteousness, were mighty in word and in deed, and who have implanted their impress so broad and so deep on the Christianity of Scotland, that time is only bringing it into greater distinctness, and which we may well believe will reach forward beyond time present to that glorious future when the Church militant shall be merged into the Church triumphant.

CHAPTER IV.

EASTERN BREADALBANE AND AIDIN.

AIDIN was the patron saint of eastern Breadalbane. The site of his church and churchyard is to be found at Innis-Aidin, on the north bank of the Tay, not far from where it issues from the loch, and at no great distance from the present parish church of Kenmore. He also set up an establishment, probably of monks, at an island near the east end of Loch Tay, and which was then called Eilean-Aidin. Here, it is said, he was frequently visited by Donald Breac, who, according to Fordun in 632, according to others in 629, ascended the throne of the Gaelic kingdom, and with whom he was on terms of the closest friendship. To this friendship may, perhaps, in part be attributed his selection by the elders of the Celtic Church for the Northumbrian mission. The reminiscences of him do not bulk so largely in eastern as do those of St Faolan in western Breadalbane. The reason is obvious—the stay of Aidin in the former being only temporary, whilst the real life-work of Faolan was found in the latter.

Aidin was a member of the Ii-an community, from whence, about the earlier part of the seventh century, he came to eastern Breadalbane. The very date we cannot give, but we know that in the year 634 he was called away, as already stated, at the request of King Oswald, to Northumbria.

As he could only preach in Gaelic, he laboured under a serious difficulty in prosecuting his work amongst the Northumbrians. In the pages of Bede we have the interesting picture presented to us of Aidin preaching, and Oswald, who had learned to speak the Gaelic language fluently when in Scotland, carefully interpreting to his commanders and ministers. Notwithstanding this serious drawback, he met with abundant success, and being joined by other Scottish missionaries, reclaimed the Northumbrian nation to Christianity. The wonderful reverence, amounting even to the superstitious, with which he was regarded, contributed in no small degree to this end.

The venerable historian has depicted the character of Aidin to us in vivid lines. Undertaking his mission expressly on the principle that his converts were to be treated as new-born babes in Christ, and therefore fed not with strong meat but milk, he exercised his authority with the utmost gentleness to their shortcomings. He had no such pity, however, on himself, but lived a life of the most austere self-denial. When not mortifying his body by hard work, he was constantly occupied with his company, whether monks or laymen, in writing or reading the Scriptures, learning the Psalms, watching, or meditating. He was singularly meek and full of peace and charity, with a mind devoid of anger and avarice. His tenderness in comforting the afflicted, and relieving or defending the poor, was wonderful, whilst at the same time he used his full authority in reproving the haughty and powerful. The Word of God was his constant guide, as he took care to omit none of the things written therein, but to the utmost of his power performed them.

Such is the glowing picture which Bede presents to us, but no sooner does his enthusiasm for genuine piety carry him into that higher unclouded region of pure spiritual atmosphere, than wretched churchism calls him back to that which is of the earth—earthy, for he adds, "These things I much love and admire in the aforesaid bishop, because I do not doubt they were pleasing to God; but I do not praise his not observing Easter at the proper time, either through ignorance of the canonical time appointed, or, if he knew it, being prevailed on by the authority of his nation not to follow the same." Having said so much to quiet his ecclesiastical conscience, he breaks through the bonds of grovellism, and bursts out into joyous appreciation of real goodness, where he says : " Yet this I approve in him, that in the celebration of his Easter, the object which he had in view in all he said, did, or preached, was the same as ours—that is, the redemption of mankind through the passion, resurrection, and ascension into heaven of the man Jesus Christ, who is the mediator betwixt God and man."

It is almost a pity to bring a shadow over this bright picture; but no saint, however saintly, was perfect, and neither was Aidin. His shortcomings, indeed, were those of his age and training, and, in the eyes of his monkish biographer, were excellences rather than blemishes. Still in his pages it is easy to trace them. He tells us that he practised nothing but what he found in the prophetical and evangelical writings; but it is readily seen that in one important respect his surroundings led him astray from their true import. Thus we find him perverting the injunction "to do unto others as we would wish others to do unto us," into, his doing to others *much more* than, either in truth or in justice, he could wish others to do unto him ; and so by an exaggeration in an opposite direction, making the Word of God of none effect by his blind, and, in the circumstances, selfish misinterpretation. His self-denial having passed the bounds of scriptural precept, merged into self-seeking, and violated the rule of the precept that we have duties to ourselves as the co-equivalent of our duties to others. In this unwarranted way we find him wearing out his bodily health and strength by continually traversing town and country on foot when he could equally well do so on horseback. His charity, again, was indiscriminate, and not without a painful tinge of vainglory; for thus we find him bestowing a valuable horse with his trappings, which King Oswin presented him with for his journeys, on the first beggar that asked alms of him. The very rules of common courtesy were set at defiance by him; for we are told that, when he and his clerics sat at meat with kings, no sooner was their hunger appeased than they rudely departed, under pretext of zeal for work and extreme sanctimoniousness. In all this it is impossible not to see, as already stated, a so-called *self-denial* which has passed into *self-seeking*. And what was the result? That by assuming this false perfection, the unlearned and uncultured multitude were led to exalt him to a pinnacle of fetishism, and to ascribe to him wonderful and miraculous gifts, which, being adopted as genuine by the monkish historians, have brought exceeding contempt on Christianity.

Still, with all his shortcomings, Aidin is a noble figure, standing out in all his real self-denial, meekness, zeal, and undoubted sincerity; reverenced and loved in his life, and no less revered after his death by those whom he had taught to live and to die in the hope of a glorious immortality.

After seventeen years of hard work he passed into his rest, and was buried in the land of his adoption. There, however, all his bones were not to lie, for Colman, the last of his successors, when departing to his own church and country, in consequence of Northumbria having gone over to Roman Catholicism, carried with him some of them, and left part in the church where he had presided. Doubtless this church was Innis-Aidin.

So lived and died the patron saint of eastern Breadalbane.

CHAPTER V.

FORTINGALL AND ST CEDD.

THE lovely and fertile vale of Fortingall is in the form of a triangle, its base at the western running into a narrow valley at its eastern end. It is about three miles in length, and about three-fourths of a mile at its greatest breadth. Through it flows the river Lyon, which shortly after leaving it joins the Tay about three miles below Loch Tay. The side of the triangle to the south is formed by "*Druimmin*," or "the Ridge of the Feinne," a hill of no great elevation, which separates Fortingall from the eastern end of Loch Tay and the upper end of the Tay valley. The side to the north is formed by a range of hills which recede backwards until they culminate in the remarkable peak of *Schiechallion*, which separates Fortingall from Bunrannoch. The base on the western side is formed by the truncated point at the eastern end of the great Benlawers range, which runs longitudinally to the west, and separates Glenlyon on the north from central Breadalbane on the south. At the southern angle of this base a narrow pass leads to Loch Tay, and at the northern angle an extremely picturesque pass threads its way into Glenlyon. At a point betwixt these angles the Romans pitched their camp, the traces of which are still clearly discernible. On seeing themselves encircled with hills and mountains, with to them no apparent outlet, it is said that they exclaimed, "Behold the end of the world!"

The notable event in the civil history of Fortingall was the repulse of the Romans by the Feinne. It has been said that a decisive battle was fought here, in which the Romans were defeated. I cannot believe that such was the tactics of the Feinne. The remains of their strongholds are still to be seen on both sides of the valley; and I conceive that they occupied these hills, taking refuge when attacked in force by the Romans partly in these forts and partly by retiring to the mountains behind. From thence at every suitable opportunity they sallied forth, cutting off supplies, and attacking the enemy—but so as not to risk a pitched battle, harassing them on every side, and carrying on a guerilla warfare on terms to them the most favourable. Be it in this way or by a general battle, one thing is certain, that the Romans were driven back, and never got any further footing within the bounds of the Gaelic kingdom.

The early ecclesiastical history of Fortingall is interesting. There are traces in it of three Celtic saints—Fiachre, Ciaran, and Ceode. Some doubts may exist as to the first two of these having been at Fortingall, the evidence only amounting to a probability. There can be no doubt as to the other having been there. I will now consider the claims and history of each of them.

1. *Fiachre.*—It was the custom of the Celtic Church missionaries, wherever they succeeded in making converts, to fix upon a pool wherein they baptized them, and which in consequence was named after the missionary. Now there is a pool at Fortingall, on *Alt-odhar*, called *Linne-a-Fhiachre*. At a much later date than that now referred to, and under another church, Fortingall became a vicarage; and it has been supposed—not altogether without probability—that the proper name of the pool is the "Vicar's

Pool." This, however, is contradicted by the pronunciation, which in this case would be "Linne-a-Bhiocar," and not "Linne-a-Fhiachre," as it undoubtedly is. To this I can testify, being intimately acquainted since infancy with the pool and its surroundings. Not far from the pool, at Balnald-beg, there is a remarkable boulder of great size, called "Clach-ma-luchaig." This is plainly a gross corruption of the name. It has been supposed to mean "*Clach-moluag*"; but there is not even a distant probability, that I know of, of St Moluag ever having been at Fortingall. My idea is, that the real name is Clach-*Mofuttack*. The Celtic name of *Fiachre* is *Futtack*, which, with the usual honorific "mo" before it, becomes *Mofuttack*. It is also perfectly easy to account for his having been at Fortingall, as we know that from Ireland he went to the continent of Europe, where he became the patron saint of St Brie in France; and also that in his journey he passed through Scotland, and left enduring monuments there of his success as a Christian missionary. We find him at Dunbarney in this county, and at Nigg, on the opposite side of the Dee from Aberdeen. The ancient name of this latter parish was *St Fiacres;* there is also a well and a burying-ground called St Fithocs, and the bay near which the church stands is called St Fickers. There is, therefore, every probability that he Christianised at Fortingall on his way to Dunbarney and the east coast. There is one other circumstance which connects Fiacre with Fortingall, and which naturally accounts for his having found his way there, that his tutor, St Conan, is commemorated in the parish of Fortingall, at Kilchonan in Rannoch. He died in the year 670.

2. *St Ciaran.*—As to a St Ciaran being commemorated at Fortingall, there can be no doubt. We have two *Dal-ciarans*, fields of Ciaran; *Ath-a'-chiaran*, his ford;

Poll-a-chiaran, his pool; and *Cladh-a-chiaran*, a burying-ground dedicated to him. There are a number of St Ciarans mentioned in the Irish calendars, but which of them is commemorated in Fortingall we have no sufficient means of judging. I have not been able to ascertain that any day was held sacred to him.

3. *St Ceode*, who is undoubtedly the patron saint of Fortingall. We have his residence at *Tigh-nhao* or *Tigh-n-naomh* (Duneaves), "the saint's house." Betwixt the house and the river is his field *Dal-mo-cheode*. At *Tigh-na-sraid*, on the opposite side of the river, we find his monumental stone or slab, *Leac-mo-cheode*. His market, Feille-mo-cheode, is held on the 21st day of August (9th O. S.). There is another market held on the 6th and 7th of December, now called *Feille-caite*, but as to which there is a vague tradition, that, for the convenience of the district, it was shifted backwards a month. If this tradition is well founded, it would place the market day originally on the 7th of January, which is Ceode's day. It would also appear that he did not confine his ministrations to Fortingall alone, but evangelised in the neighbouring districts, for at Foss, on the other side of the hill, we have *Poll-cheodan*, where, doubtless, he baptized; and at Urlar, above Aberfeldy, there is *Lòn cheodan*, or his meadow. It is worthy of note that a separate part of the parish of Fortingall is here, but whether Ceode attached it to the central seat of his labours we cannot tell.

The question is, Who was this Ceode? For my own part I have no doubt that he was the same person as St Cedd, who in the year A.D. 653 was constituted bishop of the east Saxons.* My reasons for so believing I will now give. This Ceode or Cedd, who was English by birth, had a brother called by Bede Ceadda or Chad, who from early life was closely associated with him and afterwards with

* Bede, E. H. b. iii. c. xxii.

Aidin. We are told that Chad in his youth led a monastic life in Ireland.* It is not mentioned that Cedd was with him, but from what follows it seems certain that he was. Chad expressly and Cedd by implication are stated to have been disciples of Aidin,† and seeing that he was at this time a member of the community at Ii, it is but natural to suppose that they came there from Ireland, and more particularly so as we find them soon afterwards associated in Perthshire. The continued residence of Cedd in these Celtic monasteries is strangely established by an undesigned coincidence mentioned by Bede.‡ At the synod held at Streaneshalch in A.D. 664, regarding the time of keeping Easter, Cedd was so proficient in the Gaelic language as to be able carefully to interpret betwixt the Celtic and Roman churchmen. Except to one who had for some time lived amongst a Gaelic-speaking community, this would be an impossibility. On leaving Ii the three friends are found in Perthshire, at short distances from each other, Aidin being *Naomh* of Innis-Aidin or Kenmore, Cedd of Fortingall, and Chad of Logierait.

Aidin's connection with Kenmore, and Cedd's with Fortingall, has been already shown. Chad's with Logierait is also quite definite. We have his place of residence, and his glebe at Grandtully on the south side of the Tay, called

---

* Chad, when in Ireland, is by Bede associated with Egbert, as having both "long led a monastic life there together when they were youths." If this Egbert was the same who afterwards became abbat of Iona, there must be some error in dates, as, according to Bede, he was born in 639; and it is impossible, if Chad was contemporary in age with him, that he could as a youth have lived long in Ireland, been a disciple of Aidin, who died in 651, and a brother of Cedd, who is described as venerable, and also died in 664. Perhaps some other Egbert may be meant.

† Bede, E. H. b. iii. c. xxviii.
‡ B. iii. c. xxv.

Croit-Chad, and at the same place the remains (*larach*) of a chapel, which must undoubtedly have been his. His market was until lately held at Logierait on the 22d of August. At one time there was *Fuaràn-Chad*, or Chad's well, on the hillside behind the church. The place is still pointed out, but the water has disappeared, in disgust, as tradition has it, at the market being dropped.

In perfect consistency and in full confirmation of the preceding narrative, we find the three friends again associated in Northumbria. It was natural that they should accompany Aidin on his removal there, as they were natives of that country, and as we know from their after lives, keenly solicitous for its advancement in the love and practice of the Christian faith. Two years after Aidin's death, Cedd became successively missionary to, and then bishop of, the east Saxons. Chad became abbot of Lestingau, bishop of York, and then of Lichfield.

We have already seen that part of Aidin's remains were carried back to Innis-Aidin. It is also extremely likely that part of Cedd's remains, or his relics, were brought back to Fortingall and deposited under *Leac-mo-cheode*. The tradition of the district has it that he was buried there. This of course is an impossibility, but from the analogy of the kindred cases, we would expect this other. From Dempster's "Menologium Scoticum" we find, under date March the 2d and 3d, that Chad's "reliquiæ" were brought to Scotland and deposited at a place called *Dundrain*. There is a place called *Dun-Droighne*,* on the opposite side of the river Tay, a little to the westwards of Croit-Chad, and where tradition has it that some much venerated grave existed. The grave is not specifically attached to Chad's name, but still it seems not at all improbable that it is the *Dundrain* referred to.

With regard to Cedd's market at Fortingall on the 21st,

* Or " *Tom-Droighne.*"

and Chad's at Logierait on the 22d August, it may be mentioned that they were evidently named in honour of the saints, although not held on their days. It was a necessity all over the Highlands to have markets about the middle of August for the sale of lambs, and these markets were undoubtedly fixed at that period for this special purpose. This accounts for their not being associated with the saint-days.

Betwixt these two brothers their existed an affection of the deepest and strongest kind, and yet in character they appear to have been to a large extent unlike.

Cedd was possessed of burning zeal, but also of decided mental power, prudence, self-reliance, and determinate character. This is manifest from the trust reposed in him whenever new fields of Christian enterprise opened up; the permanent success of his efforts; the high dignity to which he was advanced; and the reverence in which he was held. Thus we find that on Paeda, king of the Mercians or middle Angles, being baptized, and asking instructions for his people, Oswy, king of Northumbria, selected Cedd as one of four presbyters notable for their erudition and good life to undertake this mission. Shortly afterwards, on Sigebert, king of the east Saxons, becoming a "citizen of the eternal kingdom," and requesting Oswy to give him some teachers "who might convert his nation to the faith of Christ and baptize them;" he sent to the province of the middle Angles for this "man of God," and giving him another presbyter for his companion, sent him there. Such great success followed his labours, that, as already stated, he was ordained bishop over that people. A striking trait in his character was his intense love to his native country. Although bishop of the east Saxons, he was wont to visit Northumbria in order to "make exhortations." He also founded there, amongst the Deiri, the monastery of Lestingau, of which he made his brother Chad abbat, and in the working and success of which he took the keenest interest. With all this, however, there mingled other traits of character not so desirable. He had the lust of power, and the unhallowed propensity of ecclesiastics, to bend to their unwarranted authority the social, spiritual, and civil rights of others. Thus we find him, shortly after his appointment as bishop, magnifying his office, and adding to his dignity by ordaining under him presbyters and deacons, a thing not in accordance with what we know of the usages of the Celtic Church. Another instance still more clearly illustrates this. Having excommunicated an east Saxon earl, he forbade all who would give ear to him, to enter within his house, or to eat of his meat. The sequel we give in the words of the ancient historian. "The king made light of this inhibition, and being invited by the earl, went to an entertainment at his house, and when he was going thence the bishop met him. The king dismounted from his horse, trembling, and fell down at his feet, begging pardon for his offence, for the bishop who was likewise on horseback had also alighted. Being much incensed, he touched the king lying in that humble position with the rod he held in his hand, and using his pontifical authority, spoke thus : I say to you, forasmuch as you would not refrain from the house of that wicked and condemned person, you shall die in that very house." And of course so he did. There is one sad blot on Cedd's character. In the hour of its sad calamity, when the royal favour was withdrawn from it, and when its adherents were presented with the alternative of conformance to the Roman Church, or banishment from England, he, unlike Colman and many others, deserted the Celtic Church and went over to its rival. This was in the year 664. After this his life was but short, for that same year or soon after, coming to his monastery of Lestingau, during a time of pestilence, he was seized with that mortality and there died. Bede of course does not say so, yet we can scarcely conceive but that his latter days were clouded by the breaking up of his connection with that church, round which so many of his tenderest remembrances twined; to which his bosom friend clung with such unbending affection, and in which he died. It is true that his tendencies towards spiritual domination and priestly authority would naturally attract him towards the only church where these can find a legitimate resting-place. Still, giving him the full benefit of this doubt as to his motives, the time of his doing it was pitiable, and sorely depresses him in the estimation of the leal-hearted and generous.

Of the three friends Chad at last remained alone. Like all feeble men in like circumstances, his life henceforth, in the higher positions to which he was called, became a mere imitation of those robuster spirits whom he loved so well. His piety was of that sapless kind, without sustaining strength, which could initiate no individual action, and which—except in cases where the reminiscences of his departed friends came to his rescue—yielded itself to any stronger will. Thus we not only find him forsaking his church, but terrified by the upbraidings of Archbishop Theodore of Canterbury, displaying his flunkeyism in the most helplessly abject manner.* No more vivid idea of the sickly cast of his piety can be had than in his continuous dread of the day of judgment. Every passing blast of wind set him begging for mercy, whilst a thunder-storm drove him to the church, to prayers, and reciting of psalms, till the weather became calm. "For," we are told, "the Lord moves the air, raises the winds, darts lightnings and thunders from heaven, to excite the inhabitants of earth to fear him, to put them in mind of the future judgment." It reminds us of the experience of our childhood, when, after an evening of

* Bede, b. iv. c. ii.

doleful chanting at Dugald Buchanan's hymn of judgment or the like, we went trembling to bed in case we would be awakened by the terrific soundings of the last trumpet. Still, though imperfect and in some cases painful, evidently such as it was, this piety of his was real and genuine, and teaches us that in the Father's house there are many mansions; mansions for those weak ones who, although often bringing His cause into contempt, yet really and truly love Him, and after their manner serve Him; as well as for those strong ones who are more completely armed for fighting in a nobler and better manner the battle of truth, faith, and righteousness against error, unbelief, and unrighteousness. That Chad's piety was thus genuine is evident from the high value put upon it by the best of the monks, and which they have shown by the halo of miraculous credulities with which they have surrounded his departure. To priesthood in general this rhapsodical flaccid piety seems to be the most congenial, and it is evident that the historian believed in its genuineness. It is notable that the manlier Cedd receives no such supernal approbation. In truth, later monkish appreciation, like modern poesy and eclecticism, goes out more kindly towards "sweetly reasonable" muddlehood than towards that which is more worthy of manhood.

There is something extremely attractive in the love and lives of these two brothers. Our first glimpse of them is in their Northumbrian home drinking in the bruit, that a great wave of quickening religious power was sweeping over Ireland; and then taking up their staves and wending their pilgrim way to that land of the western sea. From thence we follow them, as, spreading their sails, they come to that lonely isle in the Atlantic, where at that time the torch of pure gospel truth burned so brightly. Here they met with one towards whom their deepest affection went forth and clung with an enduring grasp, which death alone on the earthly side, and not even death on the heavenly, could sever. Once more we see them on pilgrimage, burning with ardour to spread their Redeemer's kingdom, and now companioned by their soul-friend (Anam-charaid), whose zeal equalled their own. Onwards we follow them as they tread amidst the rugged and savage peaks of Glencoe, across the heathery moors of the Blackmount, by the verdant sides of Beinn-D'oran, celebrated in Gaelic poetry—and notable for its bloody battle, its antlered herds, its pure and sparkling springs of living water, and the cooling balm of its green water-cresses; then on through the windings of Glenlyon, and its glorious pass with its boiling floods and steeply rearing mountains, until at length is reached Fortingall, encircled with its ring of hills, and smiling in its sequestered beauty. Here, in that lovely nook formed by a bend of the Lyon, and which still bears his name, Cedd reared his wattled house, and prepared for his peaceful and blessed onset. Chad moved eastwards until he came to the fertile slopes of Strathtay and Grandtully; whilst crossing *Druimmin* to the south, Aidin pitched his resting-place at that spot, enshrined in poetry by Burns where he says:—

> "The meeting cliff each deep sunk glen divides,
> The woods, wild scattered, clothe their ample sides;
> Th' outstretching lake, imbosomed 'mong the hills,
> The eye with wonder and amazement fills;
> The Tay meandering sweet in infant pride,
> The palace rising on its verdant side;
> The lawns, wood-fringed in nature's native taste;
> The hillocks, dropt in nature's careless haste;
> The arches striding o'er the new-born stream
> The village glittering in the noontide beam."

In these scenes, where all the loveliness of what is at once grand and softly beautiful in the aspects of nature seems to be combined, these three servants of the cross fought a good fight, and amongst our fierce and impetuous, but warm-hearted and susceptible forefathers, planted that seed of gospel truth which has never since been utterly blasted. Once more the scene changes, and we see the two brothers under the leadership of their soul-friend, in their native land, battling and battling successfully for the cause of their Master, and the welfare of immortal beings. Then comes the mortal end; Aidin first passes to his rest, then Cedd, and lastly Chad. If in any case we can almost pardon the miracling of the old monks, it is, in that at least appropriate episode, when they profess that one of them saw the spirit of Cedd descending from heaven with a company of angels, and taking back with them to the realms of glory that of Chad. I doubt not that these three spirits, so loving and yet so diverse when on earth, but knit to each other in bonds so strong, are now in still closer harmony singing together the song of the Lamb around the Father's throne.

CHAPTER VI.

GLENLYON AND ST EONAN.

GLENLYON is the longest glen in Scotland. In length it is about thirty-two miles, whilst its greatest breadth does not reach half a mile. On both sides of it are steep hills and lofty mountains, towering up to 4000 feet in Benlawers on the south, and to 3300 feet in Carn-liath on the north. At one period the cleft of the glen was a succession of lakes with short reaches of river betwixt. Whether by convulsion, by the gradual wearing down of the rocky barrier in the pass through the action of the water, or what is more likely, by both causes combined, these lakes were run out, and the glen assumed its present aspect. There now only remains one small lake near the west end. Its earliest name was the Gleann-dubh, or Dark Glen; the river being called the Dubh Uisge, or Dark River, probably from its colour. There are traditionary stories variously told of how it came to be changed into the Li'uinn, and the glen into Gleann Li'uinn, one of which may be seen in General Stewart's sketches. None of these, however, seem to be well-founded. The name I conceive to come from *lighe*, pronounced *llè'a*, a flood, and *abhuin*, a river. This is most descriptive, as from the length and narrowness of the glen, the absence of lakes except the small one at the west end, and the size of the torrents swiftly running down the steep mountain sides, this river is very quickly flooded, and when thus, rushes onward with fearful rapidity. It is most probable that the change of name occurred when the lakes were emptied, as this must have completely altered the character of the river, for in its former state the gradual filling up of so many lakes, before it could come into a condition of spate, would have rendered a sudden flood impossible, except in the rare case of these having previously been almost at overflow. If this meaning of the name be correct, then the fact that the tradition of the district was perfectly cognisant of the change, shows that this catastrophe must have happened at a comparatively recent period, and this is confirmed by another tradition, which affirms that at one time the Lyon, when issuing from the pass at Fortingall, flowed through a different and much higher channel (see the new statistical account of Fortingall Parish, by the Rev. Robert M'Donald). If the occurrence took place in distant and pre-historic ages, such traditions of it would have been impossible.

The original inhabitants of the glen were *Feinne*. We have the evidence of unvarying tradition to show that it contained the central authority of one of the strongest septs of this race, and this is abundantly confirmed by the monumental and other remains. Thus we have the very old saying, "Tha da chaisteal deug aig na Feinne an gleann dubh crom nan garbh chlach"—"The Feinne have twelve castles in the dark crooked glen of rough stones." The sites and remains of all these castles (or cashels, the word being the same) are still identified. One of them commanded the pass at the western end, and another that at the eastern end of the glen. The seat of civil authority was at Cashlie, situated about twelve miles from the upper end. The castle of the chieftain or ruler was here, and its ruins may still be seen, showing it to have been a circular building, with dry-stone walls of great thickness. Within a short distance were three other castles of a similar structure. These castles formed refuges to which all the inhabitants fled in times of danger, but they may also have at other times been to some extent used for residence. It is undoubted that the more immediate retainers of the chieftain would form a small colony whose houses surrounded the fort; but whether he himself lived within, or had a dwelling-house adjoining, it is impossible to say. About a mile to the westwards we find their watching-place, called "Suidhe' einne." It is on the top of a knoll rising up in the midst of the valley which commands a view of both sides, and also an extensive prospect for long distances both up and down the glen. Betwixt this watching-place and the castle we have what is now called "Shian Chambuslai," but which is probably one of the Feinnian sepulchral mounds, and which if opened might perhaps give us up some ancient relics. There are the remains of a round tower on its summit. We have also at Cashlie a hugh stone placed above others, and wedged underneath so as to keep it off the ground. That it was the work of the Feinne seems undoubted, but as to what was its object we have no tradition to guide us. This tribe of Feinne occupied not Glenlyon alone, but the other surrounding districts. The most notable event in their history was the repulse of the Romans at Fortingall. In this, however, they would have the assistance not only of tribes from other parts of the Gaelic kingdom, but most likely also from the Cruithnich. At a much later period a large part of Glenlyon passed into the hand of Norsemen of the name of M'Dougal, who came into it from Argyleshire. As a strange incident illustrative of the hereditary transmission of physical qualities, it may be mentioned that the captain, or "portair" of one of their war vessels married amongst the Feinne of Glenlyon, and that almost all his descendants, even to this remote generation, and who have the subname of Clan-a-Phortair, have a peculiarly short conformation of the last finger of both hands.

The chief seat of religious worship in Glenlyon was at Balnahannait, situated about six miles above the pass. The word Annait is of great interest, as it closely connects the Gaidhill of Scotland with the cradle of the race in Asia. We find it under different spellings—Annait, Annat, Innit, Andat, Andate, and Annand; but of these the first two are by far the most common. The object of worship was Annat, Innit, or Anaitis, the female representative of Anu, the chief or great God of heaven. Her worship prevailed over the three great ancient kingdoms of Western Asia—the Persian, the Assyrian, and the Khetan or Hittite. The wide extent of the two first of these has been known for long, but it is only from the results of late modern research that the extent of the latter has been brought to light. At one time it extended from the Euphrates to Lebanon, and from the south of Palestine to the Euxine, the Colchians and the Urumians who inhabited Western Armenia and Cappadocia being tributary to the Khetan king of Carchemish (*Times*, weekly edition, 30th January 1880). We can from this conceive how widespread this worship must have been in Western Asia. Just as with ourselves, we have present proof from the names of places in Armenia of her ancient worship having existed there. Thus Mr Bryce tells us that on the very spot where now stands the church of the monastery of Etchmaidzin, there had stood a shrine and "image of the goddess Anahit."[*] We have an interesting record of the same kind from as far to the eastwards as Kashmir, where Mr Wilson informs us places of worship are termed Annats (Abode of Snow, *Blackwoods' Magazine*, May 1875). The monumental inscriptions afford ample proof of the worship of this goddess in Assyria. Dr George Smith gives us the

[*] "Transcaucasia and Ararat," Bryce, p. 300.

following from one of the most notable inscriptions, "and Ishtar went to the presence of Anu her father, to the presence of Anunit her mother, and said, Father, Izdubar hates me, &c." (Smith's "Assyrian Discoveries," 1875, p. 177; see also Bunsen for proof of her worship in Persia and Assyria). Smith came to the conclusion that Anunit was the wife of Anu the God of heaven. That Annat was worshipped by the Khetans we have proof of from the monuments of Egypt, where we find that Seti I. invaded Palestine, and amongst others attacked and took Kadesh, a city of the Khetans. "The local goddess of Kadesh was Anata or Anaitis, the bellona or goddess of war of the land of Canaan, and she appears armed with spear and shield when introduced into the worship of Egypt" ("Egypt from the Earliest Times," by Dr Birch, p. 116, 117). Coming now to our own Gaelic kingdom, we find places called Annaits spread broadcast over the whole of it, and associated by invariable tradition with the ancient worship. The old mythologists Origen and Dio, who use the term Andat and Andate in perfect accord with this, tell us that she was a heathen goddess of the Caledonian Gaels. We have some monumental remains to the same purpose, as, for instance, we find an obelisk in the parish of Strath in Skye, called "Clach-na N'Annait," or the Stone of Annat. We have also a rite, which in my younger days was universally observed once a year, in which I have often taken part, and which undoubtedly formed part of the same worship. It was celebrated after this fashion on the evening of the first Tuesday of the first spring moon. The whole household having assembled, a priestess was appointed, who required to be either the eldest or youngest unmarried member of a family, and who during the ceremony had to maintain perfect silence. She then proceeded to make cakes of oatmeal and eggs. One of these was large and contained symbols, which when ready was cut up and used for purposes of divination.

Of the smaller ones some were eaten and some used for dreaming upon. In fact it was the reverberation of the ancient worship of the queen of heaven by cakes. What connects it with our goddess is the name of the cakes, which were called Bonnich-Innait, or the Cakes of Innait, and the Tuesday sacred to the rite "Dimairt-Innait," or the Tuesday of Innait. A still further coincidence is to be found in the name Annand, by which one of the battle sprites or goddesses of the Gaidhill was known. We have therefore mythology, tradition, topography, monuments, and rites, alike testifying to this ancient worship amongst our ancestors the Feinne or Gaidhill. Combining all these evidences, the relationship betwixt the early races of Western Asia, and the Feinne of the Scottish Gaelic kingdom, is fairly and fully established.

The question has been put, What was the difference between the worship at the Annaits and the clachans or circles of stones? No perfectly satisfactory answer that I know of can be given, as neither written nor unwritten history throws a full light upon the subject. It may be that the ordinary worship was performed at the one, and special or extraordinary at the other; an example of which we have in the Jewish temple and synagogue, the offering up of sacrifice being restricted to the former, and prayers, teaching, and praise alone practised at the latter.

In Christian times there were certainly places of worship at some of the Annaits. This is in accordance with the custom which led the Christian missionaries, for the purpose of not unsettling the minds of their converts by too violent a breaking up of old associations, to plant the churches in close proximity to the ancient places of worship (Bede, b. i. c. xxx.). Through time in the Celtic Church, Annait or Annoit came to mean the parent church or monastery presided over by the patron saint, or which contained his relics.

That Balnahannait in Glenlyon was a place of Celtic Christian worship is put beyond a doubt by the discovery in August 1870 of the very old Celtic Church bell, which may now be seen in the Antiquarian Museum in Edinburgh.

Christianity if not introduced into the glen, was at least placed on a firm and lasting footing by its patron saint Eonan or Little Hugh. Who he was, or whence he came, we can't tell. There is a tradition, which is not improbable, that he came to Strathfillan with Congan and Faolan, and there separated from them, taking Glenlyon for his field of missionary effort. The constant association of his name with its religious history, the unfailing record of his work and success, handed down from generation to generation, together with the distinct traces of his personal work, put his life and labours in the glen beyond doubt. At Baile-a-Mhullin-Eonan (Milltown of Eonan) we have the place where he resided, and a meal-mill, the original of which was built by him. It is only at a late date that it was allowed to work on the sixth of October, the saint's day. We have also close at hand an island named after him, with a pool beside it, where probably he baptized his converts, and some miles further down the glen, at Craigiannie, the stone at the side of which he knelt, when by the efficacy of his prayers he stayed the progress of the plague in its devastating journey up the glen. The glen tradition also bears that he died at Baile-a-Mhullin, having previously directed that the coffin containing his mortal remains should be carried eastwards until one of the duil or loops of wythes placed under it for steadying the bearers broke. It was consequently borne down Glenlyon, through Fortingall, and onwards through Appin of Menzies, until one of the duil broke at the place thenceforward called Dul or Dull. Here he was buried and a church built over his grave, where afterwards a monastery was instituted, and where now stands the Parish Church of Dull. His Féill was until lately held at Dull on the sixth day of October. Some eminent archæologists identify him with Adamnan, the biographer of Columba, but in my opinion on utterly inadequate proof.

At Kerrowmore there is a burying-ground called Cladh-Bhrainnu, and the site of an old chapel beside it. This chapel was built about the 12th century by one of the M'Dougals, who owned the upper part of Glenlyon. He dedicated it and the burying-ground to St Brandan, the patron saint of his native country, Lorn in Argyleshire. It was built to replace a chapel on the opposite side of a morass, which M'Dougal's lady objected to as wetting her feet and dress when she went to public worship.

At Invervar, a few miles further down the glen, there is a Cladh-Ghunnaidh. We find in King's Kalendar, under date 13th April 858, a Saint Guinoche, who is represented by Camerarius as having contributed by his prayers to Kenneth M'Alpine's victory over the Picts. I have been unable to find any circumstances connecting him with Glenlyon, further than this "Cladh" and a well in its neighbourhood.

It is a remarkable fact, adverted to already in a more general reference (page 38), that the traces of the Druidic worship should be found to such an extent in this glen, whilst the peculiarities of Roman Catholic worship should have almost if not entirely vanished.

CHAPTER VII.

FAOLAN OR ST FILLAN OF WESTERN BREADALBANE.

BETWIXT Loch Tay on the east, and the march of the county near Tyndrum on the west, a distance of twenty miles, extends Glendochart, famous as the scene of Faolan's life-labours. Near the eastern end of the glen, and not far from the head of the loch, stands Killin, the market-town of the district.

Glendochart is not celebrated for terrific and rugged mountain scenery, like Glencoe or the Coolins, but has a grandeur of a different character. Lofty mountains, clothed here in heather, there in green; cloudy shadows frequently flitting across their sides; and serried ridges of multiplied lines and forms of varied beauty, and along their sides strangely shaped stones and boulders of rocks deposited by the ancient glaciers. Along the strath there are stretches of river, its course broken occasionally by lochs; sometimes wending its way slowly and solemnly through green meadows, and anon rushing along, as at the celebrated bridge of Dochart, at Killin, with fire and fury. Not the least notable object in the scene is Benmore, rising near the centre of the glen, and rearing towards the clouds that glorious profile of grandeur and beauty which is seen from far.

Killin, or Cille-fheinne, the burial-place of the "Feinne," for romantic beauty of its own kind is probably unrivalled. The mountain ridge, extending all along the north side of Glendochart, and dividing it from Glenlochay, suddenly about a mile above Loch Tay, comes to an end, and, with a very steep break, drops to the plain ; and there, on its southern side, in a long and picturesquely irregular form, extends the village of Killin. Standing on the summit of this break, and looking eastwards towards Loch Tay, a scene of wonderful beauty spreads itself out grandly before us. In front stretches the plain of Finlarig and Auchmore, and beyond, the loch, reposing in its deep bed amidst the mighty mountains. From the glen on the right, in a straight course, and with boiling current, as if hurrying on to lose itself in the great lake, rushes the River Dochart. From the gorge on the left issues the River Lochay, and then slowly winds and wanders through the plain until it joins the Dochart immediately above the loch. Strath and glen, wood and water, colours varied from the light green of the pastures to the dark green of the pines, the grey of the rocks to the rich purple of the heather, and above all, the glorious mountains stretching their peaks and ridges of never-ending majesty and splendour all around, combine to form a picture which, once realised by a spirit sympathetic with God's works of nature, becomes to that spirit a joy for ever.

Such then is the country in which of old our father in the Christian faith, *Faolan*, was called on to labour.

About the end of the seventh or beginning of the eighth century, Kentigerna, a native of Leinster, and a very devout woman, sailed from Ireland, along with her brother Congan and her son Faolan. Their object was the glorious one of extending the knowledge of our Lord Jesus Christ, and eternal life through Him, to their brother Celts of Scotland. They landed in the north, and after spreading the gospel at Lochalsh, Kentigerna, Congan, and Faolan came to a place in the upper parts of Glendeochuy (now Glendochart) called Siracht (now Sraithudh in Gaelic; Strathfillan in English), where a place for building a *basilica* was, it is said, divinely pointed out to Faolan and his seven serving clerics. Kentigerna did not remain in Strathfillan, but passed onwards, for the sake of contemplation, to Innis-Chailleach, in Lochlomond, where she died in the year A.D. 733 or 734.

In the interval betwixt his landing at Lochalsh, and coming to Strathfillan, Faolan spent some time amongst the monastic community on the Holy Loch, presided over at that time by St Mund. It seems probable that he had taken on him in Ireland the vows of a Deoraich, or itinerant eremite, and that on the expiry of these he took up his permanent abode at Strathfillan.

It is utterly impossible that monkish biographers could write the life of an eminent Christian without interlarding it with miraculous legends, and Faolan has not escaped these. He was born, as we are told, with a stone in his mouth, which caused such contempt in his father, that he had him thrown into a neighbouring pool or lake. There he remained for a year, fed and sustained by angels. Through a divine revelation, he was found by Bishop Ibar playing with the angels. Lifting him safely out of the lake, the bishop took him to himself, baptized him, and instructed him in the knowledge of God. "But after his youthful years had been thus passed, he betook himself to the most devout Abbot Mundus, from whom he received the monastic rule and habit. In this monastery, that he might more easily labour in divine contemplation, he secretly constructed a cell not far from the cloister, in which on a certain night, while the brethren of the monastery announced by a little servant that the supper was ready, the servant kneeling and peeping through a chink in that cell to see what was taking place, saw the blessed Faelanus writing in the dark, with his left hand affording light to his right hand. The servant wondering at the occurrence, straightway returned to the brethren and told it. But blessed Faelanus having this made known to him supernaturally, and being angry with the servant that had revealed his secret, by divine permission, a certain crane which was domesticated in the monastery, picked out the eye of the servant and blinded him; but the blessed Faelanus, moved with compassion, and at the instance and supplication of the brotherhood, straightway restored the eye of the servant."

Passing from these and such like, let us see what Faolan's real work in Glendochart was—a work so great that his memory is endeared to every native of Breadalbane, whilst his name is a household word to us from our infancies. It was threefold, but all three united in the one end of bringing his brother men to a belief in the blessed realities of a true faith in the Lord. First, and above all, he preached the Gospel. These Celtic missionaries were strictly "Gospellers." They passed much of their time in studying, reciting, and transcribing the Scriptures. There are still pointed out three spots where Faolan read the book and instructed the people. In Strathfillan, at the upper end of Glendochart, the place where afterwards was built the monastery; half-way down the glen, a place called "Dun-ribin;" and at the lower end, close to Killin, "Cnoc-a-bheannachd." Second, he encouraged the cultivation of the land and the improvement of agriculture. This is clearly evident from the fact that he and the other Celtic missionaries in this district, wherever they settled, built meal-mills for grinding the corn. Faolan's mill was built at Killin, and it is a striking proof of the veneration entertained for his memory in the district, that it is only recently that the mill was allowed to be worked on Faolan's day. Third, he set up fairs for the sale and barter of the produce, thus introducing the principles of political economy. Faolan's fair was established at Killin, and is still held there in the month of January.

It thus appears that these Celtic Church clergy introduced enterprise and civilisation as subsidiary means to the progress of their great work of Christianisation. It is intensely interesting to contemplate these olden missionaries under the light thus thrown upon them. A most pleasant sight are they. No mere austere and repulsive clerics, but men of common sense, freely mingling with their fellow-men; preaching and teaching faithfully the Gospel, but also ploughing land, sowing and reaping crops, building mills, grinding corn, and setting up fairs. Sometimes as I pass along the market-place of Killin, I picture in my mind's eye the old Christian gentleman moving, as no doubt was his wont, in midst of his own fair; every head uncovered before him, every eye filled with love and gratitude to him, every difficulty submitted to his award, and every semblance of vice hid from his glance. And thus Faolan, "having converted many to the faith of Christ," and "full of happy days, migrated to Christ on the fifth of the Ides of January, and is said to have been honourably buried in the said church, which is in Strathfillan, and there he reposes" ("Brev. Aberdeen").

There is a strange tradition in the district in reference to his burial. He died, it is said, from home, somewhere about Strathearn. The Breadalbane men, of course, proceeded to bring his body to Glendochart. They carried it across the mountain-pass of Larig-Hele until they came to a place, still pointed out, where Glendochart opens out upwards and downwards. The day being very warm, they laid down the coffin and rested themselves. During their rest, a violent dispute arose between the men of Upper and Lower Glendochart—the one desiring to have him buried at Strathfillan, the other at Killin. But on looking round, what was their amazement to find two coffins, exactly similar, instead of one. The dispute was at once solved—the one party took the one coffin to Strathfillan, and the other party the other to Killin, rejoicing greatly in the miraculous gifts of their departed saint.

Before leaving the miraculous powers of our saint, it would be unpardonable to pass over the "Holy Pool," to which was imparted through him the gift of curing madness. At one time numbers resorted to it, and even within my own recollection two women were plunged into its healing waters; but now, when the steam-whistle disturbs its solitude, all faith in its efficacy has come to an end. The process which the patients underwent was as follows:—On the first day of the quarter (o.s.), after sunset, they were plunged overhead into the pool. They were instructed to take up three stones from the bottom, and walking in Deas-shuibhal (sunwise) three times round each of the three cairns on the bank, to throw a stone into each. They were then conveyed to the ruins of the chapel, and left there tied all night in their wet clothes. If found unbound in the morning it pretokened cure. It is also said that at one time Faolan's bell was, during part of the ceremony, placed upon the patient's head. I can quite conceive that in some cases the journey, change of air and scene, together with the powerful hydropathic treatment, may have helped to effect a cure.

The circumstance which of all others has brought Faolan into notice is, the veneration in which his relics were held by Robert the Bruce. Bruce had caused the case containing, as he believed, the arm or other relic of Faolan to be brought to his camp before the battle of Bannockburn. The miracle which followed is thus related by Bœce (Bellenden's translation) :—" All the nicht afore the batall, K. Robert was right wery, havand great solicitude for the weil of his army, and micht tak na rest, bot rolland all jeopardees and chance of fortoun in his mind; and sum times he went to his devoit contemplatioun makand his orisoun to God and Sanct Phillane quhais arme as he believit set in silver wes closet in ane case within his palyeon; traisting the better fortoun to follow be the samin. In the mene-time the cais chakkit to suddanlie but ony motion or werk of mortall creaturis. The Priest astonist be this wounder went to the altar quhaire the cais lay; and quhen he fand the arme in the cais, he cryit here is ane great mirakle; and incontinent he confessit how he brocht the tume cais in the field, dredaned that the rillik suld be tint in the field quhair sa gret jeoperdies apperit. The King rejosing of this mirakill, past the remanent nicht in his prayaris with gud esperance of victorie." It was to the "mirakle of Saint Phillane" that the king alluded in his speech before the battle, after that the Abbot of Inchaffray had said mass "on ane hie mote, and ministret the eucharist to the King and his Nobillis." Bruce had an intimate connection with Glendochart. One of his battles, Dal-righ, or the king's field, was fought there, and traditions still exist amongst our old people connected with his wanderings in the glen. It was no doubt what he learned at this time of the fame of St Fillan that filled him with such veneration for his memory, and gave him such trust in his posthumous powers. Bruce endowed the chapel of St Fillan with the lands of Auchtertyre in the neighbourhood, he also gifted the patronage of Killin to the abbat and convent of Inchaffray, but with the condition that the whole fruits and profits thereof should be applied towards keeping up the service of divine worship at Strathfillan.

It is necessary to mention, as extreme confusion exists on the subject, that our Faolan and "Faolan of Ratherran" (or Dundurn), after whom the village of St Fillans, at the east end of Loch Earn, has been named, are not the same. The latter lived a century (or a century and a half) before the former. He was not a Celtic churchman, but a follower of St Ninian and the Roman Church ; and lastly, his day was on the 20th of June, whilst that of the Breadalbane Faolan was on the 9th of January. St Fillan of Ratherran was called "Faolan-an-lobhar," or "The Leper," also "The Stammerer." He was of the race of Angus, son of Nadfraech, *i.e.*, King of Munster. The church of Aberdour (Fife) was dedicated to him. Some have erroneously appropriated the district of Killin to this saint instead of Faolan of Glendochart. Not to speak of the whole tradition of the district, the fact that "Feill Faolan," at Killin, is held on the 9th January, and not on the 20th June, is quite decisive on the point.

Unlike these other saints, we have no Cummian or Bede to give us a glimpse into Faolan's inner being. What were his natural characteristics, and how these were modified, purified, and strengthened by grace we can't tell. All we know is that he was one of those intellectual and spiritual giants amongst his fellows, who leave their impress on something more durable than rock, even on human spirits ; and that after the lapse of a thousand years, we of Western Breadalbane, at the remembrance of him and of his works, rise up and call him blessed.

CHAPTER VIII.

FAOLAN'S RELICS.

I. THE CROZIER, LOCALLY KNOWN AS THE FARAICHD AND COIG-MHEURACH.

THE history of this celebrated relic has become so well known that the most cursory reference to it is only required. The fullest information can be got in "historical notices" of it by Dr Stuart in the "Proceedings of the Society of Antiquaries of Scotland," Vol. XII. I need merely state that the hereditary keepers of it from the "tyme of King Robert the Bruys and of before" were the Dewars of Glendochart, and that their special privileges as custodiers thereof were confirmed to them by letter of James III., dated 1478. Dr Stuart also makes out a strong case in favour of its being the relic which so encouraged Bruce the night before the battle of Bannockburn. It has lately been returned to Scotland from Canada, where it was taken by one of the Dewars, and can now be seen in the Antiquarian Society's Museum in Edinburgh.

In the record of the proceedings of an inquest held regarding it, at Kandrochit, Killin, on 22d April 1428, it is called the *Coygerach*. This word has given rise to a variety of meanings, all of which are entirely fanciful. That which Dr Stuart supports is the most so of any, as it is flatly contradicted, by the signification of the word from which he derives it, in Western Breadalbane, and indeed every Gaelic-speaking district with which I am acquainted. He says it comes from *coigreach*, a stranger, and goes upon a far-fetched idea that some pilgrim may have brought it from abroad, whence the name. It is a pity that such a high authority should countenance this imaginative style of interpreting Gaelic names. The word *coigreach*, or stranger, is never applied either to an animal or a thing, only to a person, consequently it can't be applied to the crozier. In Breadalbane it was known as the *coig-mheurach*, or five-fingered, no doubt from the fingers of the left hand being placed on it, when the cleric blessed, according to Celtic custom, with the uplifted fingers of the right hand. On its return from Canada, Peter M'Gibbon, an old village archæologist, asked me to have it examined to see if it had a five-fingered design upon it. I consequently wrote to Mr M'Lachlan, who got Sir Noel Paton to examine it, but without finding such a design. The incident, however, shows how undoubtedly this designation was attached to it. It is the only one which can show any usage in its favour, and therefore demands acceptance. The ridiculous term *quigrich*, invented by some south-country scribe at James's Court, is an abomination to all real Gaelic scholars, there being no such letter as Q in the alphabet.

By far the most common name for it in Breadalbane is the *faraichd*. The custodiers are called Deorich-na-faraichd; the chapel where it is said at one time to have been kept, and the ruins of which may still be seen at Auchlyne, was called Caipal-na-faraichd; and we have two crofts in Glendochart, one at Auchlyne, and the other at Suie, called Croit-an-deor-na-faraichd. It is said that the chapel was burnt, and that one of the Dewars rescued the faraichd at the risk of his life. I can give an appropriate meaning of this word, but it must be borne in mind that I have neither tradition nor usage to support it, and therefore it must be taken for what it is worth. The mission of the faraichd was that of a protector or guardian. It watched over the interests of Glendochart whether in peace or in war. Now we have a verb *faire*, to guard or watch, which has the same pronunciation, and from which, as far as suitability is concerned, it may well be derived. It has at least no insuperable objection to it, in the very application as Coigreach has. But after all it is guess work.

The name Deoraich or Dewar came through time to be an official designation. The duties seem to have been something akin to those of a modern church officer, and more especially the taking charge of relics, such as croziers, and ringing of the bells. The name, however, was originally *family* and not *official*. The latter was derived from the former, and *not* the former from the latter. This is very evident from the history of the Dewars of Glendochart, who were always a family, and possessed their official rights and privileges from being members of that family. The origin of it is of great interest. In the records of the inquest held in 1428, we are told that "the office of carrying the relic had been conferred in heritage on a certain ancestor of Finlay Iore, the present bearer by the successor of St Fillan, and that the said Finlay Iore was his successor in the said office,"—who this successor of St Fillan was, what office he held, or at what date it happened, we can't tell. Dr Stuart says that this successor must have been "one of the Comharbas, or heirs of the saint, in the monastery," but in fact we have no proof either that there was a monastery at Strathfillan, or such a thing as a Comharba. We are simply told that Faolan built a *basilica* or stone church there, and at the time of Bruce there was nothing further than a mere chapel, until he got it erected as a priory. It is true that in the 12th century, or four hundred years after Faolan, we find a lay abbat of Glendochart, but when this abbacy was established, or where it existed, we do not know. Indeed, traditional traces point to Auchlyne and not to Strathfillan as the ecclesiastical centre. The lands of the Macnabs* were also confined to the lower parts of Glendochart. One thing seems certain, that the Dewars were descended from some Deoraich, or wandering eremite, who on the expiry of his vows settled down, married, and had a family. I do not consider it improbable that Faolan himself may have been this Deoraich. We find in him the requisites of an eremite of this class. Thus we find him leaving his own country, and coming to the north of Scotland, where the traces of his evangelising are still to be found, and afterwards we find him as far south as Kilmun. That at this period of his life he was under vows, is shown by his erecting an eremitical cuile or hut, for purposes of retirement and contemplation. On leaving Kilmun and coming to Strathfillan, he dropped his wanderings and settled down as permanent minister of Glendochart. There is nothing inconsistent with Celtic Church custom and usage in his entering into marriage, and it would be a most natural thing for a successor of his in the office of ministry to hand over the custody of his relics to one of his own family. Deorich-na-faraichd lived at a place called Eyich, or Euich, opposite Faolan's basilica, on the other side of the river. At a period subsequent to that of Bruce, they possessed some of the lands of Auchtertyre, which were gifted by him to the priory. In fact, these Dewars had at all times a most intimate connection with the church at Strathfillan.

II. FAOLAN'S BELL.

This relic was stolen from Strathfillan by, it is said, an English tourist, but happily has been recovered for Scot-

* *i.e.*, Descendants of the abbat.

land, and is now in the Antiquarian Museum. It is of the orthodox Celtic Church shape, but instead of being, as is usual with these, hand-made and rivetted, it is of cast metal.* As we find that after Dewar became an official name, part of their duties consisted of the custody and ringing of the bells, and as in their case the official privileges sprung from the family, it is probable that originally they were the custodiers of Faolan's bell as well as of his crozier. If so, the name Euich casts some light on another part of their duties. The meaning of it from the Gaelic word *'eighich*, is *proclamation*. At Euich in Strathfillan, we have the traditional *Tulaich-na-h'eighich*, or knoll of proclamation. It therefore seems to follow that the Dewars were the public heralds, and in all likelihood used the bell when calling attention to their announcements.

III. HEALING STONES OF FAOLAN.

There are eight stones so designated, which from time immemorial have been preserved at Faolan's Mill at Killin. They are preserved in a niche in the wall, and at each renewing of the mill such has been duly made for them. They are small stones in the rough, evidently taken from the bed of the adjoining river. One of these stones has two holes in the centre of it, and another, now broken, evidently had the same. Mr Anderson suggests that these were sockets for the spindle of the upper mill-stone; and after his kindly showing me some stones in the Museum of a similar kind, I quite concur with him. One of the stones, however, has the segment of a circle cut in it, which seems to point to something more ancient than Faolan. Peter M'Gibbon, the village archæologist already referred to, tells me that he remembers when the whole inhabitants turned out on Faolan's day and put clean straw under them.

* For full information as to all known Celtic Church bells, I would refer to Mr Anderson's forthcoming "Rhind Lectures."

CHAPTER IX.

THE FEINNE OR GAIDHILL.

THE characteristics of the *Gaidhill* have been, and are at this moment, grievously misunderstood, which results from some of our neighbours, the *Gall*, taking in hand, from the slenderest real knowledge of us or our language, to give a full and correct estimate of our hereditary qualities, our genius, our springs of action, and, in fact, of our whole actuality. One gentleman has undertaken to show, from our romances and parables, that at the comparatively recent period at which these were invented, our forefathers were in that state associated with the "missing link," when they "would feel more at home with a fox planning some depredation, than with a Hegel or a Huxley contemplating the meaning of the universe" ("Transactions of Gaelic Society, Inverness," vol. viii. p. 92). We have the same thing in the folly of travellers and missionaries, fancying they had plumbed the inner life of savage tribes when they only knew the surface, and the still greater folly of scientists building scientific laws on such statements. A notable instance is to be found in the conclusion arrived at a few years ago, with a sneer of old-wifehood towards all who doubted, that there were many heathen tribes who had no idea of a God—a conclusion which further inquiry has about, if not entirely, exploded. It is only those who thoroughly know their language, who have long lived with them—long enough and intimately enough to imbibe their lines of thought, feeling, and special idiosyncrasies—who know their history, written and unwritten, with their usages and customs, who are acquainted with both their ancient and modern literature, and who have reached the root of their religion, that can venture to lay bare the peculiar characteristics of the Gael. It is under the impression that some of the most salient points in our mental being have been not only overlooked, but misstated, by strangers to us and our ways, that I make the following observations :—

Before proceeding, however, a few observations as to our ancient bardic literature is absolutely needed. It consists of three kinds, two *spurious* and one *genuine*. The two spurious consist, first, of romances or fairy tales, chiefly Irish, in which the old Gaelic heroes are elevated to the level, not of Hector and Achilles, but to that of Jack of the Bean Stalk or his namesake the Giant Killer. They are of a much later date than the genuine, and except for perhaps a few incidents and references, historically of less than no value, as by their extravagance in fact and language they obscure the real. Second, ancient poems completely transmogrified by the priests into conformity with sacerdotal claims and pretensions, and which, therefore, are of no value. The real old Feinne or Gaelic poetry we find in the remains of Ossian, collected by M'Pherson, whether we look upon these as interpolated with other matter or not, and in the collections of Gillies, Stewarts, and others.* It is noteworthy that Lord Webb Seymour and Professor Play-

---

* For my part I believe that the Fionn-geal lived and his son Ossian sung during the 3d century, the former coeval with the Roman Caracalla and the Irish Cormac-Mac-Art ; and that this is borne out alike by ancient poetry and annals.

fair, when travelling in the Highlands inquiring into bardic remains, were cautioned against these later tales, which ascribed miraculous feats and the powers of giants to the heroes of the Feinne (see Appendix to Report by Committee of Highland Society, appointed 1797, to report on Ossian's remains). No one really saturated with a knowledge of Gaelic language, literature, history, usages, and idiosyncrasies, can have any difficulty, I conceive, in distinguishing betwixt the real and the spurious.

I will now call attention to a few of the characteristics of the Scottish Gaidhil :—

1. He is both imaginative and ethical. His tales and *sguelachds* abound in the fanciful, ascribing reason and speech to animals, and inventing incidents quite beyond the region of the actual. In all of them, however, the end and purpose is ethical. In fact they are parables, throwing a strange light on the then ethical development.

2. The Gaidhil is *emotional*. He does not, however, wear his feelings on his coat sleeve, but looks with supreme contempt on those who go about turning themselves inside out, under the least excitement, for the inspection of all and sundry. Their emotional nature is only reached through the intellectual—a fact well known to the best Gaelic preachers, who never attempt to stir the inner being of a Gaidhil by the mere sentimental. When this emotional nature, however, is fairly roused, its intensity is profound. On this subject much nonsense has been spoken and written, as if the Gaidhil was a creature of mere impulse and sentiment.

3. The Gaidhil intellectually is thorough in his thinking. No proposition can find favour with him which is not founded on intelligible premises, expressed in plain understandable language, supported by honest inductive reasoning, and carried out to its legitimate end. Most distasteful

and repugnant to him are the dogmas of "sweet reasonableness," involving utter contempt of logic; or sublimated words, such as we find in modern poets and philosophers, which require a telescope to ascertain their sense, if sense they have. Most amusing it is to see their devotees expending days or months after an idea, and when they find some mystified resemblance to one, necessitating a volume to elucidate it, or further to mystify, as the case may be, rejoicing as over great spoil. Nothing so clearly illustrates this trait in the mental constitution of the Scottish Gaidhil as his fervent attachment to the Pauline, or, in modern language, Augustinian or Calvinistic theology. Now, whatever estimation this system is held in, all will acknowledge it to be the most purely logical of all systems. Yet it is the system most congenial to the Gaidhil. Coming from systems to particular doctrines, there is none so hateful to some of our southern neighbours as a belief in God's sovereignty or predestination. Now, in our statement of it, it is both logical and reasonable. We do not believe, as is falsely imputed to us, in fate or necessity. We believe in two things seemingly irreconcilable—God's sovereignty, without which we can't conceive of him as God, and man's free agency. We believe in them, first, because they are in that region where such difficulties are logically expected, that is, in a region above but not contrary to our reason; and, second, because they are two facts. This we have first convinced ourselves of. We believe in them just as we do in two forces upholding nature—to us seemingly irreconcilable, negative and positive electricity, or centripetal and centrifugal force, not because we understand them, but because they are facts. Further, facts of our infancy as irreconcilable then, are now easily reconcilable; and just so, when we get nearer to God, these seeming irreconcilables of our later age will be as easily reconcilable.

Our southern friends will not allow this; they will listen to no reasoning; on hearing predestination mentioned they shut their ears, and open their mouths in the most abusive and senseless language, and call us all manner of bad names.* On the other hand, when fairly stated, it proves conclusively my proposition, that the Gaidhil is a reasoning being, and believes on logical principles only. I never can forget a statement by one of the greatest of Gaelic preachers, now no more, which illustrates this subject, viz., that in his experience, a Highlander fairly aroused to religion as a reality of present and future life, never had peace until he argued out with himself the foundation point if there was a God, and, therefore, a legitimate authority to impose a law.

I have dwelt rather fully upon this subject, as there is an impression generally abroad that the Gaidhil is led to a large extent by his feelings, and without depth in his inductive reasonings, and thoroughness in thinking out a subject.

I have spoken of the Scottish Gaidhil alone; and it may be objected to my position that the Irish Gaidhil does not think for himself, but is led by his priest. This, however, results from his having accepted the premise that the priest has a portion of divine powers entrusted to him. Holding this premise, nothing can be more thoroughly consistent than the Irish Gaidhil's deduction from it. I venture to prophecy from the Gaelic characteristics, that, when he comes to doubt of his premises, we will see an ecclesiastical revolution in his ideas.

4. The Scottish Gaidhil lives under a constant sense of the oneness of his present and future life. This is no new idea, but is found in the most ancient poetry;

* See "Contemporary Review," vol. xxi. p. 437, for painful and pitiable example.

thus Silric consoles himself at the thought of Binnbheul's death :—

> "I will sit by the fountain cold,
> On the top of the heights in the wind;
> From the heath in the still noon-day
> My beloved will speak to me.
> Come, my Binnbheul, on the breath of the breeze
> Come, like a gleam on the tufts of the cairn,
> At silent noon, when thy spirit shadows mine,
> Thy voice let me hear, O my Binnbheul!"

This is confirmed by the Roman historians, who state, not only that the Gaidhill believed in a future state, but that this belief delivered them from the fear of death and incited them to bravery. There is no warrant in the ancient poems for the notion that they believed in the transmigration of souls. This belief in immortality, and that the life hereafter is simply a continuation of the life here, is still most characteristic. I have heard old people speaking of their change, as they call it, with the greatest composure and satisfaction, indeed, with many it forms a favourite subject both of thought and conversation.

5. The Gaidhil is *musical;* but his intense delight in music is not simply as an æsthetical luxury, but as an inspiring means of interpreting and intensifying to him the highest poetic thoughts and feelings, combined with the aptest words for expressing these thoughts and feelings. This was exactly the mission of the ancient bards. Whether they raised their impassioned lays as the Feinnian combatants with naked bodies and bared broadswords advanced to battle, and with intensest impetuosity hurled themselves against their adversaries; or whether they sung their lays within the festive hall, their object was, by the sublimest language wedded to the boldest or tenderest music which their highest inspiration could reach, to fill their countrymen with all that was

noble, tender, and heroic. The bard was wonderfully equipped for delivering his glowing message. He had not only the gifts of poetry and song in their highest form, but he was also a patriot and a hero, and spoke and sung from the heavings of the grandest and mightiest conceptions stirring within his own spirit. We can conceive the scene when "Fionn," having returned from battle to the "hall by the waves," and partaken of the "bounteous feast with the flowing shell," thus addressed his bards :—

> "Ye voices of Cona, of high swelling power,
> Ye bards who can sing of her olden times,
> On whose spirits arise the blue panoplied throng,
> Of her valiant hosts, who were mighty and strong,
> My bards raise the song."

And can we not see the bards rapt in ecstasy as the mighty deeds of their fathers swept in power through their spirits, and then in prophetic frenzy seizing their harps, and pouring forth words and music that roused and stirred to the very depths of courage and exalted fervour the being of the Gaidhil. Even music purely æsthetic, such as that of the pipes, has a mighty power over the Gaidhil, by its association with his deepest impulses of love, family, or patriotism—those hidden but profound idiosyncrasies which have for ages swayed with entrancing force his inmost being. Pipe music does not stand alone; in its composition it is united with some incidents or deeds ever memorable, whether these were grievous, joyous, or daring, and hence its power. It was, indeed, a descent when the pipes, as an incentive to bravery in the hour of battle, had to be substituted for the bard; but still the descent is not so great as it looks, when this law of association is taken into account. Lord Byron knew this well, and gives voice to it in his ode on Waterloo, where he says :—

The Feinne or Gaidhill.

> "And wild and high the 'Cameron's Gathering' rose!
> The war-note of Locheil which Albyn's hills
> Have heard; and heard, too, have her Saxon foes.
> How in the noon of night that pibroch thrills,
> Savage and shrill. But, with the breath which fills
> Their mountain-pipe, so fill the mountaineers
> With the fierce native daring which instils
> The stirring memory of a thousand years,
> And Donald's, Evan's fame rings in each clansman's ears."

We have an apt example of the same by Kenneth M'Kenzie, where he says of the pipe :—

> "Bheireadh i air ais gu fonn
> An cridhe dh' fhas gu tursach trom,
> 'S chuireadh i spiorad's gach sonn
> Gu dol air am gu spadaireachd.
>
> Fhuair i 'n turram thar gach ceòl,
> Cuiridh i misneach's gach feoil,
> Togaidh i gu aird nan neoil,
> Intinn seoid gu baitealach."

Which I may translate—

> "To joyance it would swiftly bring,
> Each heart that grief and sorrows wring,
> Each champion's spirit it would fire,
> And heroism great inspire.
>
> O'er every music is its fame,
> The patriot's courage to inflame,
> And high as heaven to upraise
> The hero's soul in valiance."

In olden times, when the clans engaged in battle, the bards, with their harps in their hands, in order to raise them to the greatest heights of valour, rushed through the ranks, and in words the most thrilling sung the deeds of their forefathers. In still more ancient times the warrior imagined, in addition to this, that his war-sprites went wheeling on lightning wings above his head, uttering the most frantic shouts. The harp and recitative were afterwards superseded by the pipes. The demeanour of the Gaidhil in the hour of battle, as this has come down to us by tale, ode, and tradition, is strange and remarkable. To realise it aright we must remember that men did not then fight in masses with weapons of precision in their hands, deadly at long distances, but that each warrior fought with his good broad-sword, not only for his nation's weal, but for his own individual life. His joining in the combat was, we are told, often preceded by a strange nervous excitement, called by the ancients *crith-gaisge*, or quiverings of valour. This was succeeded by an overpowering feeling of exhilaration and delight, called *mir-cath*, or the joyous frenzy of battle. It was not a thirst for blood, but an absorbing sense that both his own life and fame and his country's good hung upon his efforts, coupled with a self-consciousness that, as far as a bold arm, a resolute will, and undaunted spirit could do and dare, all was well. Grandly does the king of great mountains describe this mir-chath, when he says :—

"Well do I remember the champion,
Said the king of the hills and woods,
And how, with *heroic frenzy, in battle he consumed the fight.*"

This "mir-chath" may still be witnessed on the few occasions in modern warfare when the Highland soldier has a chance of charging with the bayonet. Then may be heard that shout which has often wakened the echoes of our mountains, and ever precedes an onset which no foe has yet dared to meet.

APPENDIX.

I.

IT has been said that the Feinne were not a people, but a militia, who hunted or fought all summer and autumn, and lived all winter in the mansions and public-houses. This is in entire contradiction to the most ancient Feinne poetry and lore, where we find that love, courtship, marriage, family life, and affection for their children, form, along with heroism, the most prominent characteristics of the race. The authorities for this militia statement are some stories, already referred to, of the fairy tale kind, evidently of a comparatively recent date.* They have not even the weight of the romance which goes under the name of Geoffrey's "History of England." It is strange to find those who ignore all of the most ancient Celtic poetry and remains gravely stating this militia fiction without the semblance of doubt as to their authorities. There is, however, some amount of truth in the assertion, and it is this—that the Feinne set apart some of themselves to be what we may call their fighting men. In ordinary circumstances the fighting would fall on them, but in extraordinary emergencies every available male would be called out.†

* See "Pursuit of the Gilla Dacker," translated by Joyce in his "Old Celtic Romances."
† See "Tacitus's Agricola," c. xxix.

In the poem called "Tiantach mor na Feinne," we are told—

"Teachaireachd thainig gu Fionn,
Teachaireachd chuir rinn gu truath,
Comhrag dluth d' Fiannaibh Fheinn."*

"News came to Fionn, news that grieved us sore, that a battle was near to the *Fiannaibh* of the Feinne." From which it would appear that these Fiannaibh were the active forces of the Feinne. It will be noticed that they were part of the nation, and some married; in fact, judging from our ancient authorities, a large proportion of them were. Of course, if the whole of the Feinne were merely a militia quartered on others, it was impossible that they could be either married or a people, and must have been selected out of various tribes. The idea of their not being a people is preposterous to us, who have the reality of their being such in our chronicles, our poetry, our traditions, and inscribed on hills, rocks, and glens. Even the ecclesiastical and fairy romances that find such favour in the eyes of Professor O'Curry frequently imply a family and national life. †

II.

A question frequently arises as to whether the saints personally lived and taught in the districts which are dedicated to their memories, or whether they came to be so dedicated from the possession of some of their relics, or other incidental cause. When we find in a district the saint's place of residence, the field or croft which he cultivated, the pool where he baptized his converts, the meal-mill of which he erected the original, particular spots where incidents connected with his history occurred, and, above

---

* "Gillies's Collection," pp. 306, 307.
† "O'Curry's Lectures on Irish MSS.," p. 227 and following.

Appendix.

all, the record of his life and successful work handed down from generation to generation, and still green in the hearts of the people, we may conclude unreservedly that he personally laboured therein. Even should some of these marks be wanting, yet enough may remain to enable us to come to the same result. The traces of Aidin, Ceode, Chad, Eonan, and Faolan undoubtedly meet what is needed of these requirements. The mere facts of a church, churchyard, or market being dedicated to a saint does not necessarily imply his personal residence.

III.

It seems now to be the fashion to deduce all Gaelic names bearing any ecclesiastical significance from the Latin. Such there undoubtedly are, but the indiscriminate reference of all such is as undoubtedly wrong. The usual derivation at present of *bachall*, a crozier, is from the Latin *baculus*. I conceive that a pure Gaelic derivation has much more in its favour. Rods of virtue or potency existed long before there was a Latin language or the special usages of Christianity. They were used among the Druids by the *Ollamh*.* The Gaelic derivation is, probably, from the word *buaidh*, virtue or potency, to which is added *cuaille*, a rod or staff. *Buaidh-chuaille* would therefore be *rod of potency*. We find a crozier, assigned to Columba, termed *buaidh* only, without the *cuaille* added. It went by the name of *cath-bhuaidh*, or battle potency. This very clearly shows *buaidh* to be the root of the word. We all know the connection of shepherds with rods or crooks, and the Gaelic *buchaill*, a shepherd, may be from the same word *cuail*, with *bò*, a cow, prefixed. Another instance of misplaced Latin derivation which intimately concerns our

* See Professor O'Curry's "Lectures," p. 5.

inquiries as to the origin of the *cuiltich*, occurs in the Irish name Errigal, found in the church of Errigal Keeroque, a parish in Tyrone. The annalists spell the word *Aireagal*, and with them it means a small church, oratory, or hermitage. Joyce* derives it fom the Latin *oraculum*. He says, "It has been used in Irish from the earliest times, for it occurs in the oldest MSS., as, for instance, in the *Leabhar na h' Uidhre*, where we find it in the form *airicul*." This latter, I conceive, shows at once its meaning, which I take to be *aori-cuile*, from *aor*, worship, and *cuile;* in other words, the place of public worship, or the *cuile* used as a church by the whole cuiltich resident at one diseart, in contradiction to the private cuile of each eremite. I have no local knowledge of Tyrone, but feel some interest in ascertaining if there was a diseart there. The word "aor" may be derived from the Latin "oro," or both may come from the same source. As to *cuile* being Gaelic there can be no doubt, and just as little that in the Gaelic kingdom its translation into Latin, when used for an eremite's hut or a church, was *cella*, its original use in this connection being cuile, or dark recess, in which the Druids performed their ceremonies. As already stated, its application is not confined to a church, nor was it synchronous with the introduction of Latin, in which case there might be a show of reason in deriving it from *cella;* but both as a compound and simple word it had, long before there was any Latin in Scotland, been extensively used otherwise. In its simple form of cuile, we find it all over the country applied to recesses, whether in woods or elsewhere; and in its compound form it equally meets us at every point and in all manner of applications. Thus we have in Glendochart ardchyle, or the *high recess*, which some who go on sound alone imagine to be *high wood*. In Strathtay we have

* "Irish Names," 1st series, p. 319.

cuile-cille-a-chassie, or the recess of the steep burying-ground. At Loch Ludnaig side we have Ard-chuile-an-righ (Anglice Ardchullery), or the high recess of the king. It is situated at the end of a very narrow pass, into which the deer from immense distances were driven, and then made to pass through this cuile, where the kings of Scotland were wont to station themselves on their hunting expeditions. We have also cuile-na-moine, cuile-a-mhullin, cuile-an-shiogal, and multiplied others. In fact, it is the purest and most ancient of Gaelic.

www.ingramcontent.com/pod-product-compliance
Lightning Source LLC
Chambersburg PA
CBHW022146160426
43197CB00009B/1449